GO

DEVOTIONS FOR FAITH ON THE MOVE

tim baker

Revell

Grand Rapids, Michigan

For my family at Hope Fellowship.

//

© 2006 by Tim Baker

Published by Fleming H. Revell
a division of Baker Publishing Group
P.O. Box 6287, Grand Rapids, MI 49516-6287
www.revellbooks.com

Printed in the United States of America

Library of Congress Cataloging-in-Publication Data

Baker, Tim
    Go : devotions for faith on the move / Tim Baker.
        p.   cm.
    Includes bibliographical references.
    ISBN 10: 0-8007-5882-X (pbk.)
    ISBN 978-0-8007-5882-0 (pbk.)
    1. Devotional literature. I. Title
BV4811.B315 2006
242—dc22   2006020072

Contents

Acknowledgments

Many thanks to

My kids, my friends, my family, and the students I've met along the way in youth ministry who have allowed me to use their stories or their influence in my life as material for this project.

The entire editorial staff at Baker Publishing Group for their hard work. Jennifer Leep, thanks for your willingness to take on these books and for your unending patience.

Jacqui. Thanks for allowing me time to write this. I love you! (Psalm 126:1–3)

Introduction

I know an alien, and I'd like you to meet her.

When she was a teenager, my wife was invited to a youth group costume party. She was excited and took the opportunity to get creative. With a little help, Jacqui created the perfect costume. The whole process went something like this:

Step 1: Create a powerfully impacting and wonderfully creative costume. Jacqui considered her options. What should she dress as? All sorts of ideas flooded her mind. Finally, she settled on making herself an alien.

Step 2: Find alien materials. Using a variety of props from around the house, Jacqui was able to create a costume that she thought resembled an alien. Green hip waders and a green rain poncho for the base costume. A green mud mask and glitter for the exposed part of her face. Green shoes on her feet and hands. A headband with two green Styrofoam balls on springs (they bounced as she walked!).

Step 3: Attend the party. In the end, this proved to be the most difficult part.

Proud of her accomplishment, beaming with creativity, Jacqui loaded herself into the backseat of her parents' car, and her mom drove her to her friend's house. Convinced that her friends would go wild over her outfit, Jacqui had prepared a variety of responses—"Yes, I made this myself." "Sure, I can make your costume next year." "No, I've never done this before, and yes, I have impressed myself. Thank you very much."

The house was easily visible as they rounded the corner into the cozy neighborhood. From seven houses down, Jacqui could see the other girls piling into the house, each of them led by their parents. And every one of them was dressed like a princess.

"A *princess*?!" she said aloud. "*No one* told me I was supposed to dress like a princess."

Instinctively Jacqui lay down, hoping no one would see her as her mom drove closer to the house. "I'm not going in, Mom. Keep driving."

"You've spent too much time to not go," her mom argued. "Your costume is wonderful. You're an alien princess!" With that, Jacqui's mom stopped the car at the mailbox, right in front of the house.

Peeking just a bit (and holding down her alien bouncy-ball headband thingies), Jacqui noticed her best friend dressed like an Indian princess. In the weeks of planning, even her best friend hadn't told her that she was coming dressed as a princess.

"No way, Mom! *Please* . . . let's just go!" Jacqui said, feeling the sting of embarrassment—and feeling like an outsider.

"This is a test of your character," her mom said, looking over the backseat into Jacqui's alien face. "You're going in, and you're going to have a good time."

Resolving to impress her friends with her creativity, and buying her mom's "alien princess" scenario, Jacqui dragged herself out of the backseat and slowly walked toward the door.

One minute earlier and the bird traveling overhead would have missed her. However, Jacqui's exit from the car perfectly matched the flight plan of a bird relieving itself. Almost as if the bird was waiting for her. Just as if he had planned it. Jacqui got nailed with runny bird doo.

This was a problem. It stunk. It drizzled all the way from the top of her alien head down to her alien shoulder. Maybe her friends would buy the alien princess idea, but there was no way she could convince them that bird poop was proper adornment for an alien princess.

One quick swipe with her mom's handy wipes and the alien princess was ready for the party. And, as the night went on, she did get compliments. At a party filled with human princesses, Jacqui, the alien princess from an unknown planet, actually won an award for her creativity. She impressed her friends, and she even surprised herself. Turns out, it *was* a test of her character and strength. And oddly enough, she *passed* the test.

Have you ever felt like an alien in a world full of princesses? Ever felt like you try and try but you're still out of place? Like everyone else's invitation read one thing and yours read something different?

As we're trying to live our faith in Jesus, we *will* feel out of place. We will be persecuted. We'll struggle with our beliefs. We'll struggle with loneliness, hurt, fear, and pain. But, in the midst of our discomfort, God comforts. In the midst of our pain, God heals. When we feel pooped on, God wipes us off, tells us how important we are, and sends us back into the party.

That's the key to moving forward in your faith. Always feeling like an alien, always feeling out of place. Living like an alien in a world full of princesses. And knowing and relying on God's power and presence when the party has gotten to be too much.

This book is designed to help you live your faith even when you feel like an alien. Because this world *will* make you feel like an alien, and, in fact, you *are* an alien. When you feel out of place, insignificant, and pressed for both answers and time, this book will be your hope and help.

How Do You Use This Book?

I've put this book together so you'll be able to use it in two ways. You can pick it up anytime and read a couple of pages for your devotions, or you can begin at the beginning and devote just a few minutes each day to reading a couple of pages. Here's a heads-up on the format you'll see:

Day 1: This day might involve a bit more effort and usually asks you to write down your own ideas about a topic after reflecting on Scripture.

Days 2–5: These days generally hang out on the topic for the week and help you understand more about the topic.

Day 6: This day gives you a situation you might encounter and asks you to try to apply what you've learned through the week to the topic.

Day 7: The last day of the week, you get to have a little fun. These are usually simple activities that help illustrate the theme for the week.

Really, it doesn't matter how you use this book. Before you sit down and begin, though, here's a little advice about having devotions.

1. Find a good time. You've got to read God's Word when you're most awake and alert. Some people are alive at 6:30 a.m., and they're firing on all their cylinders. Truth is, not everyone is like that. If you aren't alert in the morning, don't have devos then. Think about when you're most alert, and give God your time when he'll get you at your best.

2. Find a good place. Everyone doesn't learn in the same way or in the same environment. Do your friends talk about how they read their Bibles before they go to bed? Have you ever wondered why you don't remember anything you read before you go to bed but your friends do? Maybe your bed isn't the best place for you to read. Give some thought to the best place for you to read God's Word. Find a place where you'll be able to focus.

3. Pray. Lots of times we talk about how prayer after devotions is important. Truth is, prayer at the beginning is important too. Before you open God's Word, remember to ask him to guide your mind to what he wants you to learn.

4. Mark where you've been. Always keep a pencil handy. Keep one in your Bible. As you read through God's Word, mark things you think are interesting. If you do that, you'll know where you've been in God's Word, and over time you'll create some valuable notes in your Bible.

The most important thing about devotions is that you have them. It can be so tough to keep a schedule of reading God's Word. It's a tough discipline! Hopefully, *Go* will help you stay consistent in your devotional life and will challenge you to live God's Word boldly. God bless you in your journey through this book and in your walk with Christ.

What's the Hurry?

DAY 1

As Jesus and his disciples were on their way, he came to a village where a woman named Martha opened her home to him. She had a sister called Mary, who sat at the Lord's feet listening to what he said. But Martha was distracted by all the preparations that had to be made. She came to him and asked, "Lord, don't you care that my sister has left me to do the work by myself? Tell her to help me!"

"Martha, Martha," the Lord answered, "you are worried and upset about many things, but only one thing is needed. Mary has chosen what is better, and it will not be taken away from her."

Luke 10:38–42

GO

Rush . . . rush . . . rush . . .

There are those weeks, aren't there? Those times when it feels like life is living us more than we are living it. There are times when things seem to move so fast that it's difficult to breathe. Difficult to stop long enough for a meal. Impossible to talk to a friend. Never any time to do anything except the urgent.

First there's school. You get up and run to the shower (if you get up early enough). Then on to campus. Classes all morning. Scarf down your lunch, then jet to more classes. Late afternoon—practice, church, games, homework, family outings. It all goes at a maddening pace, doesn't it?

Stop and think about your life for a moment. What makes you rush around? What puts you in a hurry? What things demand your time? Write the top three things that make you the busiest throughout the day, but don't include school on your list.

- _____
- _____
- _____

Now relax. Breathe. Think through your short list. I didn't want you to put school on your list because there's probably not too much about

Week 1 What's the Hurry?

school that you can control. You can't assign yourself less homework, and you can't give yourself A's on your exams. What things on your list *can* you change? Are you playing three sports and can drop one? Are you in too many clubs at school? Are you overcommitted?

The thing about life is it can get away from you. You pile all your commitments on top of each other, get involved in things, and poof! You're overcommitted, stressed.

This week we're taking an honest look at your life. We're going to look at the things that stress you out, and talk about the most important things you *should* be concerned about.

MOVE

- Why is life often too busy?
- What things could you remove from your life, making it less packed?
- How does the busyness of your life affect your relationship with God?

DAY 2

GOD'S WORD

Then the Lord said to Moses, "Get up early in the morning, confront Pharaoh and say to him, 'This is what the Lord, the God of the Hebrews, says: Let my people go, so that they may worship me. . . . But I have raised you up for this very purpose, that I might show you my power and that my name might be proclaimed in all the earth.'"

Exodus 9:13, 16

For if you remain silent at this time, relief and deliverance for the Jews will arise from another place, but you and your father's family will perish. And who knows but that you have come to royal position for such a time as this?

Esther 4:14

It does not, therefore, depend on man's desire or effort, but on God's mercy. For the Scripture says to Pharaoh: "I raised you up for this very purpose, that I might display my power in you and that my name might be proclaimed in all the earth."

Romans 9:16–17

GO

Everything in life has a purpose, doesn't it? Your toothbrush has a specific purpose. Your car has a purpose. Your textbooks have a purpose too. A textbook would never say, "Today I will be a toothbrush." Your car would never say, "Read me! I can inform you about the history of the United States!" They'd never say that because they have a specific purpose (and because they can't talk anyway). Your toothbrush is for your teeth, not your brain. Your car is to get you around, not to educate you about history.

If everything has a purpose, then you have to ask yourself, *What is my purpose? What is the point of my life? Why am I on this planet?*

I know. In a week where I've promised that you'll whittle down and stress less, asking you to consider the purpose of your life is a little much, right? Think about it. Once you know the purpose for your life, the easier you'll be able to decide which things are the most important and which aren't.

Even as a believer, you can live your life for God and still live pointlessly. You can get up each day without knowing what you're going to do with your life. You can live that way for your entire life. You can be a solid believer, a strong Christian. You can live sinless and sanctified. But you can still live without a point to your life.

Some people will tell you that all you need for life is to know God. I don't think that's entirely true. I don't think that just "living for God" is enough. God made you for a specific purpose. That purpose is certainly found in knowing him, but it doesn't end when you become a Christian. In fact, the road to knowing God's purpose for your life *begins* when you accept Christ.

How do you know the purpose for your life? Begin your discovery by answering these questions:

1. What would you jump through fire for? Everyone has one thing he or she would brave a dangerous situation to rescue.

2. If you weren't limited by time or money, what would you give your life to? What would you do?

3. In thirty years, what do you want to be known for accomplishing?

Your answers to those three questions will probably help you define part of what your purpose is.

Remember, everything has a purpose. Even your toothbrush. Even you. When we know what God made us to do, we know what things we should focus on getting done.

MOVE

- If you could guess, what is God's purpose for your life?
- What prevents you from living God's purpose for you?
- Why is it important to live God's purpose for you?

DAY 3

GOD'S WORD

Hezekiah trusted in the LORD, the God of Israel. There was no one like him among all the kings of Judah, either before him or after him. He held fast to the LORD and did not cease to follow him; he kept the commands the LORD had given Moses. And the LORD was with him; he was successful in whatever he undertook. He rebelled against the king of Assyria and did not serve him.

2 Kings 18:5–7

Now, my son, the LORD be with you, and may you have success and build the house of the LORD your God, as he said you would. . . . Then you will have success if you are careful to observe the decrees and laws that the LORD gave Moses for Israel. Be strong and courageous. Do not be afraid or discouraged.

1 Chronicles 22:11, 13

Uzziah was sixteen years old when he became king, and he reigned in Jerusalem fifty-two years. His mother's name was Jecoliah; she was from Jerusalem.

. . . He sought God during the days of Zechariah, who instructed him in the fear of God. As long as he sought the LORD, God gave him success.

2 Chronicles 26:3, 5

GO

I've talked with loads of students, so I've had the opportunity to listen to the passion of many high school and college students. I've listened to their fears about life and their indecision about what they'll be giving their lives to. Over the years, I've kept track of what I've heard and have created a list of things that students have expressed as their fears about life. Four major fears center around

- *GPA.* The speech usually goes, "If I don't do well in school, I'll get a low GPA and won't make it into my preferred college. And my parents will be really upset. And I'll be poor, homeless, and purposeless, and I'll starve." I've seen students work like crazy to get good grades because they're convinced that good grades mean a good, easy life. Actually, I think good grades have little to do with your quality of life when school is over.
- *College.* Getting into the "right" school is important. Succeeding in college is essential. The "right" school somehow means a better future. I've watched students sweat it out through months of waiting for an acceptance letter from their first-choice university only to be emotionally crushed when they don't make it in. You know, I'm just not convinced that the "right" school has a lot to do with your entire life.
- *Total and complete success.* Many students (and adults) have an unhealthy view of failure. For some reason, we've come to believe that not succeeding at something speaks volumes about our character and ability. Through the years, I've watched students try for something huge, and when they don't completely connect with their goal, they give up and allow their failure to rule their emotions. Here's the truth. There's just as much "success" in properly managing your failures as there is in handling your achievements.
- *Perfect spirituality.* I've also met countless Christian students who believe that one misstep means complete spiritual destruction. I

once knew a student who made a small spiritual misstep. For four months after committing what she thought was an enormous sin, that student regularly vocalized her spiritual failure to others and commented on how imperfect she was. Because of this girl's need for "perfect spirituality," she never could get over her mistake. She had a total misunderstanding about God's grace.

Society teaches us to hurry up, be a success, never fail, and always be perfect. In fact, the media has done an excellent job of vilifying anyone who isn't successful or makes a personal or spiritual mistake.

The truth is, God's love not only covers our failures and mistakes, it encourages us to slow down and enjoy life. We were not created to wildly succeed; we were created to enjoy God.

Achievement. Success. Prosperity. You know, our whole concept of these words is totally messed up. Success isn't an outward thing; it's an inward journey. And success isn't often found in grades, schools, or perfection. It's found in enjoying your journey. It's found in seeing your life as God sees it.

Somehow, humans have reversed the idea of success. We believe that hurrying up and succeeding at everything should come first, and then enjoying God comes after we've achieved everything we desire. However, God's design is that we enjoy him, that we let him enjoy us, and that as this mutual enjoyment is happening, we grow. No promise of success as the world defines it; only enjoying the presence of our Savior.

MOVE

- Why are you in a hurry to accomplish things?
- Why is success so important?
- What is the best way to enjoy God?

DAY 4

Then he said to his disciples, "The harvest is plentiful but the workers are few. Ask the Lord of the harvest, therefore, to send out workers into his harvest field."

Matthew 9:37–38

After this the Lord appointed seventy-two others and sent them two by two ahead of him to every town and place where he was about to go. He told them, "The harvest is plentiful, but the workers are few. Ask the Lord of the harvest, therefore, to send out workers into his harvest field."

Luke 10:1–2

"My food," said Jesus, "is to do the will of him who sent me and to finish his work. Do you not say, 'Four months more and then the harvest'? I tell you, open your eyes and look at the fields! They are ripe for harvest."

John 4:34–35

GO

In a hurry-up, get-out-of-the-way, get-it-to-me-yesterday world, I know a lady who has "slow down" perfected.

She's not upwardly mobile. She isn't trying to climb the ladder of success. She doesn't care about being a celebrity. However, by not trying to accomplish any of these things, this lady has accomplished a great deal.

She and her family lived in the same neighborhood where my wife grew up. Everyone knew each other there. Even though many families led busy lives, neighbors still talked, kids played together in yards, and cars moved slowly through the streets, wanting to see what was happening in the neighborhood.

Years ago, before they had caller ID, people could easily and anonymously make prank phone calls. When this lady got a prank phone call, she would witness to the person on the other end. She'd tell them how, if they knew Jesus, they wouldn't need to make crazy phone calls and things like that. When her neighbors accidentally called her instead of someone else in the neighborhood, she always took the time to catch up on their lives.

This lady often walked the neighborhood and talked to everyone she met. People working in their yards often enjoyed leisurely conversations with her, hearing about what was new in her life and answering her questions about what was happening in theirs.

This woman is our example of the value of living life slowly. Her willingness to take time for others and her unusual ability to ignore the ladder of success ought to be our model.

I'd like you to stop right now and consider one word. Take two minutes and contemplate this word: *slow*. Think about what it means to you. Get a picture in your mind of what the idea of slow really means.

What came to your mind? Was it skipping a few social activities so you can hang out with your parents? Did you envision not worrying so much about your grades? Did you imagine yourself taking it easy?

When I think of the word *slow*, I think of the lady who wandered the neighborhoods. I recall her willingness to stop and talk. I remember her desire not to rush but to meet, greet, hang out, and discover.

That's it. When we live life slowly, we have time to discover and enjoy.

Today God is calling us to live slowly. To discover the extraordinary around us. To wander through the neighborhoods of our lives, looking for opportunities to live like Christ.

MOVE

- Is it difficult for you to slow down? Why or why not?
- What are the benefits of enjoying your life?
- What do you think God's response is to a life lived too fast?

DAY 5

Their sight was restored. Jesus warned them sternly, "See that no one knows about this." But they went out and spread the news about him all over that region.

Matthew 9:30–31

The man went away and told the Jews that it was Jesus who had made him well.

John 5:15

Then Peter said, "Silver or gold I do not have, but what I have I give you. In the name of Jesus Christ of Nazareth, walk." . . . He jumped to his feet and began to walk. Then he went with them into the temple courts, walking and jumping, and praising God.

Acts 3:6, 8

GO

Imagine not being able to be in a hurry. Your mind wants you to hurry, but your body won't respond. Your legs, immobile. Your ability to earn a decent wage, impossible. You're willing but not able.

Actually, we ought to say, kind of willing—especially when you're talking about the lame man at the pool of Bethsaida in John 5:1–15. The Bible tells us that the guy had been waiting by the pool for years. He waited there, believing an ancient legend that, when the water moved, it was being moved by an angel. When the angel moved the water, the angel was empowering the water to heal whoever touched the water first. Being lame, the man was unable to be the first in the water and unable to be healed.

This kind of worked in the man's favor. On the one hand, he couldn't move. On the other hand, he was able to beg and therefore make an income. Since Jews were required to give to the lame and poor, he probably made at least a small amount of money just for lying around.

It was all working out fine until Jesus walked by and noticed him lying there. This man's world changed with three simple commands that charged out of Jesus's mouth.

"Get up!"

"Pick up your mat!"

"Walk!"

If you had been paralyzed for thirty-eight years, wouldn't those be astounding words to hear? Imagine the wonder of using your legs for the first time in almost forty years. Imagine how those first steps must have felt. Imagine how others might have reacted. Wonder and amazement must have filled the area around the pool. Now there was hope for others who were paralyzed, blind, lame, and broken.

And the "hurry up" here? Where is it? In the life of a man who probably wanted to be in a hurry just once but couldn't, where's the hurry in his life now?

It's pretty simple, really. After Jesus heals him, the guy demonstrates the one area of our lives where hurrying is important. Immediately after being healed, the Bible notes that the guy has a conversation with the Pharisees about the healing. This man, who couldn't be in a hurry in the past, was obviously in a hurry after his healing. Scripture notes that the guy headed straight for the Jews and told them what he'd experienced.

When we've experienced Jesus, how can we not be in a hurry? If we've had an experience, how can we not tell others about it? If we've been healed, how can we not tell others about our healing?

Ask yourself, *Am I in a hurry to tell someone about how Jesus has healed me? Have I had a real experience with the Healer? If I'm not motivated to tell others, have I really had a life-changing experience?*

MOVE

- Have you been healed? If so, of what?
- What should your response to meeting Jesus be? To keep quiet or to tell everyone? Why?
- Why should you be in a hurry to tell others about Jesus?

DAY 6

Every day they continued to meet together in the temple courts. They broke bread in their homes and ate together with glad and sincere hearts, praising God and enjoying the favor of all the people. And the Lord added to their number daily those who were being saved.

Acts 2:46–47

"Now, Lord, consider their threats and enable your servants to speak your word with great boldness." . . . After they prayed, the place where they were meeting was shaken. And they were all filled with the Holy Spirit and spoke the word of God boldly.

Acts 4:29, 31

For two whole years Paul stayed there in his own rented house and welcomed all who came to see him. Boldly and without hindrance he preached the kingdom of God and taught about the Lord Jesus Christ.

Acts 28:30–31

GO

"Tell people about the gospel! Tell people about the gospel!"

When your pastor gets on a roll like this, it's kind of difficult not to laugh. Each of his proclamations is followed by an "amen" from the people in the seats. The only thing more amusing than your pastor's "preach the gospel" rants is the congregation's chanting back. It usually happens at the end of a message, just before the closing prayer and final song. It seems your pastor does this to create a memorable closing and end with a kind of pep-rally feel. Maybe he thinks it actually inspires people to spread the gospel. Who knows.

On the way out of the building, you pass many people talking wildly about the pastor's message and his pep-rally ending. Funny thing is, you *know* most of these people couldn't care less about your pastor's end-of-the-message pep rally. If they did, you'd live in a town filled with Christians. And you don't. Something's not working.

The next day at school, you're talking to Kerri, who was at church yesterday. She makes the comment you've been thinking since yesterday morning.

"Didn't you just love the message yesterday?" Kerri's sarcasm is obvious. "Yeah, I really felt compelled to tell everyone."

"I was thinking the same thing. How many times have we heard that? I can't believe it. And everyone after . . . like they'll do anything. Like they'll say anything."

Just then Trevor sits down at the table. Apparently, he's overheard you and Kerri. "Are you joking? Pastor was right on yesterday. My parents and I went out for lunch, and we witnessed to our waitress."

You and Kerri share the same sarcastic response. "Oh, yeah. Right. We get ya."

Trevor gives the two of you an indignant look. "If Pastor hadn't told us to tell everyone about the gospel, to be in a hurry to share our testimony, I never would have said anything. You two can be as sarcastic as you want. Me and my family are going to do what the pastor said."

"Trevor," Kerri begins, "you know the people who go to our church. You know our church is just a big club. It's great that you and your family listened to Pastor's words, but the rest of them couldn't care less. As far as I'm concerned, he wasted his breath."

Trevor looks at Kerri. He's obviously peeved. "Kerri, I don't care about the people who go to our church. I'm concerned about me. Pastor convinced me that I need to tell everyone about Christ. I'm convinced. The question that's bothering me is, why aren't *you* convinced?"

Kerri looks at you for help. What will you say to her and to Trevor?

MOVE

- Is the pastor correct in the way he urges the congregation? Why or why not?
- Is it okay for Kerri to be sarcastic about what her pastor said?
- Would you help Kerri out? If so, what would you do to help her?

DAY 7

There is a time for everything, and a season for every activity under heaven.

Ecclesiastes 3:1

And do this, understanding the present time. The hour has come for you to wake up from your slumber, because our salvation is nearer now than when we first believed. The night is nearly over; the day is almost here. So let us put aside the deeds of darkness and put on the armor of light.

Romans 13:11–12

As God's fellow workers we urge you not to receive God's grace in vain. For he says, "In the time of my favor I heard you, and in the day of salvation I helped you." I tell you, now is the time of God's favor, now is the day of salvation.

2 Corinthians 6:1–2

GO

Time controls so much of our lives. Some people are more controlled by time than others. As we enter new phases of life, the level of control time has over us changes. Think for a moment how the following people might view or be controlled by time:

A baby
A student
A person beginning a career
A parent
A retired person
An elderly person

Do you feel like time controls you too much? If so, try this.

Pick a task you can do quickly and one you can do slowly. For example, you could take more time doing your homework or doing a chore around the house and less time getting ready for your day or eating dinner. Which was more comfortable for you—going fast or going slow? What happened to the things you took your time with and the things you rushed through? What results can come from being in a hurry? Maybe you're one of those people who works well under pressure, and if you are, that's great. But even though being in a hurry can sometimes have good results, it often has some pretty destructive results too.

Have you ever walked with a really fast or really slow person? It's kind of annoying. You're either running to catch up or you feel like you're caught in a frame-by-frame replay of some moment. Everyone has his or her own pace with things. Whether it's walking down the street, making decisions, or even grieving over the loss of a loved one, we all have our own pace. And when we're trying to complete a task, understanding our pace is sometimes half the battle of completing it. If you know it takes you an hour to get ready, then you allow an hour before you have to be out the door, right?

God has a *plan* and *purpose* for our lives, but have you ever considered what his *pace* for our lives might be? God wants us to approach our lives at the speed he decides. For some of us, that means attacking some things quickly and with speed. For others of us, that means moving more slowly. In the end, what matters is how God wants you to use your time. Reevaluate your priorities in your daily life, and let God decide what your pace should be with all those things and with the purposes he has for you.

MOVE

- What have you learned about being in a hurry from this activity?
- Using what you've learned from this illustration, how would you explain to your best friend the importance of slowing down and waiting on God's pace?
- How can you apply what you've learned and the truth you've discovered from Scripture to your life?

Why Should I Use My Spiritual Gift?

DAY 1

Do not think of yourself more highly than you ought, but rather think of yourself with sober judgment, in accordance with the measure of faith God has given you. . . . We have different gifts, according to the grace given us. If a man's gift is prophesying, let him use it in proportion to his faith. If it is serving, let him serve; if it is teaching, let him teach; if it is encouraging, let him encourage; if it is contributing to the needs of others, let him give generously; if it is leadership, let him govern diligently; if it is showing mercy, let him do it cheerfully.

Romans 12:3, 6–8

Now to each one the manifestation of the Spirit is given for the common good. . . . All these are the work of one and the same Spirit, and he gives them to each one, just as he determines.

1 Corinthians 12:7, 11

Our presentable parts need no special treatment. But God has combined the members of the body and has given greater honor to the parts that lacked it, so that there should be no division in the body, but that its parts should have equal concern for each other.

1 Corinthians 12:24–25

GO

Imagine that for your birthday your friends all get together and buy you this extremely nice, very expensive gift. They've all pitched in a little, and they've decided to give it to you at lunch. There in the lunchroom, they all approach you, singing and carrying this really great gift.

You're stunned. Speechless. Caught in one of those emotional moments when crying feels right. Slowly you peel off the wrapper. Before you is the one present your parents didn't buy you. It's the present mysteriously missing from your party last night, and it's the one present you were really hoping for.

The present is big but not too heavy. It's easy to handle too. Caught up in the excitement of the moment, you stand, thank your friends, and begin to beat up each of them with your new gift. You smile as you whack each of them around. Giggle as they run away from your abuse.

You chase them out of the lunchroom and down the street, swinging at them with each step. They scream and run. You can't stop laughing.

If you did that, wouldn't you be an awful person? What kind of friend would beat up his or her friends with a present? What kind of person would take a very good thing and use it for very bad purposes?

Spiritual gifts are like presents, and we often use them in all the wrong ways. When we're supposed to use them for good, we sometimes use them to hurt others. God's gifts to us are spiritual gifts, which we can use in a variety of ways. God doesn't *make* us use the gifts he gives us in one certain way. He gives us our gifts and then gives us free reign to use them however we choose.

Do you know your spiritual gift? If you do, write it below. If all you've got is some general ideas or feelings about what your spiritual gift is, write those below.

- _____
- _____
- _____
- _____

If you don't know what your spiritual gift is . . . NO WORRIES! Throughout this week we'll be learning what they are, and hopefully you'll learn what yours might be. We'll also learn why God gives us spiritual gifts, and how you can best use the gift God has given you. We'll discover the best ways to use our gifts so that we're building our friends, not whacking them and laughing all the way.

MOVE

- Why do you think God gives us spiritual gifts?
- What is the purpose of these gifts?
- What happens if we don't know our spiritual gift?

DAY 2

Just as each of us has one body with many members, and these members do not all have the same function, so in Christ we who are many form one body, and each member belongs to all the others.

Romans 12:4–5

The body is a unit, though it is made up of many parts; and though all its parts are many, they form one body. So it is with Christ. For we were all baptized by one Spirit into one body—whether Jews or Greeks, slave or free—and we were all given the one Spirit to drink.

1 Corinthians 12:12–13

After all, no one ever hated his own body, but he feeds and cares for it, just as Christ does the church—for we are members of his body.

Ephesians 5:29–30

GO

Even though your body is one thing, one piece of matter, your entire body doesn't do the same thing. Each part of your body doesn't have the same purpose. For example, your hand doesn't work well as a foot. You can't hear with your nose. Your stomach doesn't make a great face.

That's the point Paul is making in a well-known and often talked about passage in the New Testament. First Corinthians 12:1–13 and Romans 12:6–8 offer believers an opportunity to look into the mind of God and grasp what kind of gifts he gives to believers. Grab your Bible and take a few moments to read that passage.

Okay, so first things first. These two passages are where Paul lists the spiritual gifts that God gives believers. Here's what you need to do first. Make a list of all the different gifts that Paul mentions in these passages.

_____   _____
_____   _____
_____   _____
_____   _____
_____   _____
_____   _____

We could talk about a lot of ideas that Paul communicates in these passages, but we'll focus on the gifts for believers. He doesn't say that every believer has the same gift. He points out that all believers are given gifts, and the list of gifts is diverse. They're not exactly alike, and in some cases, they're very different.

Hear that? Not the same. Not cookie cutter. Not alike. Did you see yourself in Paul's list of gifts? Did you see your abilities? Did you recognize your gift? I hope so. You are given gifts to be God's unique gift to the world. Hopefully, as you read those passages, you saw an ability you have. Maybe you were able to recall a moment when you exuded wisdom, faith, or knowledge. Maybe you remember enjoying a time when you got to help or serve or give. Maybe you have a gift that's obvious but isn't on the list.

If nothing seems to stick out, the bigger question is this: What in the world do you do if you don't know what your spiritual gift is? Here are a few ideas.

First, read those passages and refer to the list of gifts that you made above. Read that list over and over. Pray through it and ask yourself, "Which of these gifts have I seen in myself? Which ones do I definitely know I do not have?"

Next, talk with people who know you. Your pastor or youth pastor. A close spiritual friend. Your parents. Ask any of these people what spiritual gift they see in you. Ask them to be very honest about what they see in you.

Third, consider taking a spiritual gifts inventory. There are several available online (do a search using the words "Spiritual Gifts Inventory" to find them). If you do an online survey, be sure to take the results to your pastor and discuss what that gift means. Or, better than taking an online survey, have your pastor give you a spiritual gifts test.

Spiritual gifts aren't supposed to be God's tiny little secret that he keeps from us. He wants you to know about the gift that he's given you.

MOVE

- What is your spiritual gift?
- How does God expect you to use your gift?
- Why should you use your spiritual gift?

DAY 3

We have different gifts, according to the grace given us. If a man's gift is prophesying, let him use it in proportion to his faith. If it is serving, let him serve; if it is teaching, let him teach; if it is encouraging, let him encourage; if it is contributing to the needs of others, let him give generously; if it is leadership, let him govern diligently; if it is showing mercy, let him do it cheerfully.

Romans 12:6–8

But everyone who prophesies speaks to men for their strengthening, encouragement and comfort. He who speaks in a tongue edifies himself, but he who prophesies edifies the church.

1 Corinthians 14:3–4

So it is with you. Since you are eager to have spiritual gifts, try to excel in gifts that build up the church.

1 Corinthians 14:12

GO

It's impossible to fall asleep on Christmas Eve, isn't it? You lie there dreaming of what you might get the next morning. A new computer. A motorcycle. All kinds of things. You look forward to the next morning like a starving man looks forward to a cheeseburger. As you fall asleep, visions of you jumping in front of the tree celebrating your major score pass through your mind.

What if your Christmas morning went a little differently? What if it went more like this? . . .

You and your family wake up Christmas morning. Your parents ask you if you'd like to start opening your presents, but instead, you want to go out for breakfast. After breakfast, you want to find an open store to go shop. Then, on the way home, you suggest stopping for a movie. You finally get home, but instead of opening your presents, you get online to IM and play games. Just before bed, your parents ask about the presents again, but you say you're tired. Maybe tomorrow. And head off to bed.

Kinda strange, huh? What would you miss out on?

Week 2 Why Should I Use My Spiritual Gift?

Or, here's another one for ya. You get to that huge pile of presents and you begin opening. The first box you rip into has a sweatshirt in it, but what you really wanted was a remote control truck. Next, you open a box of soap, but what you really wanted was that cool new video game. So you just ignore your gifts and go play with something you got last Christmas.

Wouldn't that be a waste if we didn't use the gifts that we were given?

When we're talking about spiritual gifts, here's why those crazy examples become really tragic possibilities. When God gives us a gift, it's not for the purpose of edifying ourselves. It's not for *our* enjoyment. His gifts are given to edify and build up the body of Christ. We've already read the first part of 1 Corinthians 12, but the rest of the chapter also illustrates the *purpose* of spiritual gifts. Read verses 12 through 31. There Paul explains the Big Picture—that these gifts are for the building of the body of Christ and for encouraging believers.

So, in other words, if we don't use our spiritual gift, we not only miss out on using the gift that God gave us, but more importantly, someone goes unencouraged, un-built-up, and not helped in the way that God had planned for them to be helped.

God gives us gifts so that we can help others. It's no coincidence that Paul talks about spiritual gifts right before he discusses the idea of love in chapter 13. I think he does that because he knows that too often we forget to use our gifts in love.

And here's the huge bonus: using your spiritual gift means doing what God made you to do. He gave you a gift to help fulfill who he created you to be. He made you for a unique purpose, and using the gift he's given you will bring satisfaction and contentment.

Truth is, you'll never fully be who God made you to be until you use the gift he's given you. This week spend time talking to someone who knows and loves you. Ask your pastor to give you a spiritual gifts test. Once you understand your gift and examine how you can use it, you'll be able to be a vital member of the body of Christ.

- How can you use your gift to encourage others?
- What prevents you from using your gift?
- How can your parents help you discover your spiritual gift?

DAY 4

GOD'S WORD

Therefore, I urge you, brothers, in view of God's mercy, to offer your bodies as living sacrifices, holy and pleasing to God—this is your spiritual act of worship. Do not conform any longer to the pattern of this world, but be transformed by the renewing of your mind. Then you will be able to test and approve what God's will is—his good, pleasing and perfect will.

Romans 12:1–2

There are different kinds of working, but the same God works all of them in all men. Now to each one the manifestation of the Spirit is given for the common good.

1 Corinthians 12:6–7

On the contrary, those parts of the body that seem to be weaker are indispensable, and the parts that we think are less honorable we treat with special honor. And the parts that are unpresentable are treated with special modesty.

1 Corinthians 12:22–23

GO

I've got a secret to tell you. For now let's keep this between us . . . just you and me.

For the past several months, my wife and I have been saving for an above-ground swimming pool. My being employed part-time at a church and part-time as a university professor means we've had to save for quite a while. We've had to opt for a very inexpensive model. One without any frills.

But, you see, my kids have been asking for a pool for about three years. Every spring several stores in our city display easy-to-set-up swimming pools. And every year my kids see these pools and beg for them. They beg and beg until I kindly (and firmly) explain that there is no way we can afford a pool.

Anyway, truth is, we can't afford one. But we've been saving. And recently we saved enough to actually buy one of these cheap pools. So, just between you and me, right now there is a pool in my garage. I've got it hidden from my kids. If I'm careful, I'll be able to keep it hidden from them for the next week or so. Just long enough to complete this book and get outside and set up the pool before school ends for the summer.

I'm thrilled that I can finally give my kids this gift. I'm ecstatic that I can give them the one thing that they ask for each year. I can't wait to set up the pool while they're in school. I can't wait to see their faces when they see the pool for the first time. I can't wait to play in the pool with them. I can't wait!

I imagine this is the way God feels when he gives his children spiritual gifts. God doesn't have to save up to give us gifts, but I bet he does get excited when he gives us the gifts that perfectly fit us. I imagine he's thrilled when he sees us using our gifts to edify and build the body of Christ.

God, who watches his children, looks to see if we're enjoying the gifts he's given us. He watches to see if we use what we have. He looks for the joy our gifts bring others.

Imagine my kids walking into the backyard, looking at the pool, and saying, "Dad, couldn't you have saved longer? Couldn't you have bought a better pool? Is this the *best* you could do?" I'd feel awful. I'd be disappointed that my kids couldn't find joy in the thing I'd chosen for them. I'd be sad that my kids chose not to enjoy the gift I'd given.

We need to accept the gifts God has given us. We have to use them. We have to find joy in our gifts. When we don't use our gifts, or when we ignore them, we're telling God that the gifts aren't any good, that we're disappointed in what he's given us.

I think God smiles each time he gives us gifts. I think he has complete and utter joy when we use our gifts. I think God, who took the time to create the universe, takes time to step into creation and experience joy with us when we use our gifts. I'm convinced that he's thrilled with us and loves watching us use the gifts he's given.

- What prevents you from enjoying your spiritual gift?
- Why is it difficult to enjoy your gift?
- Have you thanked God for your spiritual gift?

DAY 5

GOD'S WORD

Now I rejoice in what was suffered for you, and I fill up in my flesh what is still lacking in regard to Christ's afflictions, for the sake of his body, which is the church. . . . To this end I labor, struggling with all his energy, which so powerfully works in me.

Colossians 1:24, 29

Make it your ambition to lead a quiet life, to mind your own business and to work with your hands, just as we told you, so that your daily life may win the respect of outsiders and so that you will not be dependent on anybody.

1 Thessalonians 4:11–12

Therefore, since we are surrounded by such a great cloud of witnesses, let us throw off everything that hinders and the sin that so easily entangles, and let us run with perseverance the race marked out for us. . . . Consider him who endured such opposition from sinful men, so that you will not grow weary and lose heart.

Hebrews 12:1, 3

GO

Some people fit neatly into nice, tidy categories, don't they? They're so good at everything that it kind of makes you frustrated. These people know their gifts, and their knowledge of their gifts fuels them to accomplish, succeed, and make a difference. You probably know some people right now who impressively use their gifts far and above what you think any human can, and they easily accomplish things. There are other people who don't seem as gifted. They don't seem to have the ability to climb any ladder of success.

Years ago, a student showed up at our church one Sunday. No one knew him. He wasn't invited by a friend. This guy was cool and nice and friendly, but he didn't come off as a world changer or the kind of person who made a huge impact on anything.

The guy showed up with his guitar. Our church had never used a bass guitar in worship. Half of the people in our church had never heard of a bass guitar. When he got up to play his guitar along with the worship leader one Sunday, no one in the congregation was sure how to respond. Some had thoughts of leaving, while others started to clap along.

His first few Sundays were interesting. The long-haired, barefoot guitar player never gave up. Slowly, this young man changed our worship. He was quiet, but his movements in our church were bold and purposeful. As his guitar revved up our worship, his spirit and attitude moved through our church. Because of his enthusiasm, we added a drummer. Our worship has become more contemporary. Through the quiet efforts of this one young man, our church has boldly changed.

Through the years, the young man has changed. He still plays guitar in our worship services, but he's cut his hair, and he's started wearing shoes. He's gotten married, has graduated college, and has stuck around to work with our church as we've gone through some major changes.

Using our spiritual gifts doesn't mean making a grand entrance or creating an explosion of activity. It means working with what you know God has given you to change the place where he's called you to serve. It means obeying God's call and following his direction for how to use your gift. It means never giving up—no matter how uncomfortable you feel, no matter how strange you feel trying to use your gift. It means *using* the gift God gave you. No fear. Being totally and completely yourself.

MOVE

- What is the best way to use your spiritual gift?
- What have you affected using your spiritual gift?
- What causes you fear in using your gift?

DAY 6

For by the grace given me I say to every one of you: Do not think of yourself more highly than you ought, but rather think of yourself with sober judgment, in accordance with the measure of faith God has given you.

Romans 12:3

Now about food sacrificed to idols: We know that we all possess knowledge. Knowledge puffs up, but love builds up. The man who thinks he knows something does not yet know as he ought to know.

1 Corinthians 8:1–2

If anyone thinks he is something when he is nothing, he deceives himself. Each one should test his own actions. Then he can take pride in himself, without comparing himself to somebody else.

Galatians 6:3–4

GO

Your two best friends have never been so impossible to be around. Jaime and Nicole and you have grown up together. You've been best friends. Sleepovers. Parties. Prom. You've been through a lot. You're sisters . . . not biological but on a deeper level.

It all started when your youth pastor asked the group to take a spiritual gifts inventory. He passed out these booklets and blank forms. A week after the exam, he passed back the booklets and the forms with a kind of grading sheet attached. Each sheet told you your predominant spiritual gift along with a few other gifts you might have with a little less intensity.

Everyone looked over their forms with anticipation. This was the end of a long teaching your youth pastor had given. The idea was that tonight everyone would be helped to find a better fit within the youth group and within the church. The night went off without a hitch. Your youth pastor talked about how you could fit better in the church, and some adults there helped each of you get ideas together that helped match your gifts within the church.

It's four days later, and you're sitting with your two best friends after school. Waiting for the bus, the three of you are talking about youth group and about spiritual gifts.

Jaime has the gift of encouragement.

Sunday night lit a fire under Jaime. Since then she's been "encouraging" everyone she's close to. Unfortunately, your youth pastor's talk Sunday didn't tell you how to use your gifts, and Jaime's been left to "encourage" people by finding all their positive qualities—this includes ignoring people's really obvious negative qualities.

Nicole has the gift of helps.

Nicole isn't much of a helper, and you're sure that this is one person who failed the test. It's not that she isn't gifted or that she took the test wrong. Possibly the test just didn't measure accurately who Nicole really is. Anyway, Nicole has been "helping" people ever since the meeting Sunday night. She's "helped" by rearranging your bedroom furniture (except that you didn't want it rearranged) and by "helping" with her neighbor's flower bed (and in the process, killing the flowers).

It'd be neat to try to talk with these two. It'd be nice to help them understand a little better about their spiritual gifts. But they're not really inclined to listen to you. Besides, how much should friends help other friends understand and learn to use their spiritual gifts?

You've decided that you're going to save all your other friends the trouble and help Jaime and Nicole refine their spiritual gifts. What strategy will you use? How will you talk to them?

MOVE

- Why is it important to be careful when you use your spiritual gift?
- Have you ever tried to help someone but actually hurt them? If so, what happened?
- How does God work through us when we use our spiritual gifts?

DAY 7

Each man has his own gift from God; one has this gift, another has that.

1 Corinthians 7:7

Now you are the body of Christ, and each one of you is a part of it.

1 Corinthians 12:27

Don't let anyone look down on you because you are young, but set an example for the believers in speech, in life, in love, in faith and in purity. Until I come, devote yourself to the public reading of Scripture, to preaching and to teaching. Do not neglect your gift, which was given you through a prophetic message when the body of elders laid their hands on you.

1 Timothy 4:12–14

GO

God has given each of us gifts of special abilities, skills, or talents. As Christians, we all have them, and they're all different. We can use them all for his work and for his glory, and they're all important. But have you ever wanted to quiz God on why he chose your gifts for you? Have you ever wanted to say, "God, why couldn't you have made me a really great basket weaver instead?"

In the privacy of your own room, try this:

First, think of one or two things that you really are no good at. It could be playing the organ, painting a portrait of your dog, playing on a baseball team, or being a prima ballerina. Now take a few minutes to act out that thing. If you've ever secretly dreamed of doing something that you know you stink at, here's your chance. No one is watching (except maybe the dog), so go nuts with it.

How did it feel to pretend to do those things? What if you had really been doing those things in public? Would it have been as good as you might dream it could be?

There are some things in life that we can work hard at and be good at, and there are some things that are better left in our dreams. But there are also things that God has gifted us with. What are your spiritual gifts, and what are the things you think God has made you really good at?

How can you use them together? Take a few moments and make a list. Maybe you're a really good public speaker, and you enjoy researching the Bible. You could preach the sermon at your next youth service. Or maybe you like to help and serve others no matter the task. You could use your spiritual gift of serving at a homeless shelter or a hospital. Or maybe you are a good athlete, and you really want to spread the gospel to those around you. You could start a discipleship group with your teammates or set an example by praying before every game.

Next, think of some ways those gifts can be used even more by God. Look through your phone book or your yearbook or maybe watch the news to help you think of ideas. Then decide on three specific, doable ways to use your spiritual gifts. Keep that list in a prominent place where you're reminded often to work on completing those tasks for God. And always remember to pray for God to use your gifts for his glory, and be open to where he leads. If you're open to him, he *will* use you.

MOVE

- What have you learned about using your spiritual gifts from this activity?
- Using what you've learned from this illustration, how would you explain the importance of spiritual gifts to your best friend?
- How can you apply what you've learned and the truth you've discovered from Scripture to your life?

Why Should I Listen to God?

DAY 1

The LORD thundered from heaven; the voice of the Most High resounded.

2 Samuel 22:14

After the earthquake came a fire, but the Lord was not in the fire. And after the fire came a gentle whisper. When Elijah heard it, he pulled his cloak over his face and went out and stood at the mouth of the cave. Then a voice said to him, "What are you doing here, Elijah?"

1 Kings 19:12–13

The voice of the LORD is powerful;
the voice of the LORD is majestic. . . .
The voice of the LORD strikes
with flashes of lightning.

Psalm 29:4, 7

GO

If you could guess, what does God's voice sound like? Does he sound like an angry policeman? Does he sound like your parents? A teacher? Take a moment and think about what God's voice sounds like to you.

Now that you've got an image or sound in your mind, remember this. It's one thing to know what God's voice sounds like, but it's another thing to actually listen to his voice and do what he says. God can ask us to do a variety of things, and sometimes he asks us to do things that are so uncomfortable that it *feels* easier to just ignore him. After all, *if* we listen to him, and *if* we obey him, we can end up having to do a lot of difficult stuff.

So why should we listen to God? What are the benefits of listening to God? No doubt you've got a lot of different answers to this. Take a sec and answer this one for yourself. Why should you listen to God? Write some of your ideas below.

- _____
- _____
- _____

Consider the benefits of listening to God. Adventure? Sure. Opportunity? Certainly. An unpredictable life? Obviously. Those might be the obvious, typical answers. But what about obedience? Attentiveness? Affecting others? Those are all good reasons to listen to God, but they're probably not the ones we're most comfortable with. We love adventure, but we often don't love the obedience part.

Listening to God is an essential part of the life of the believer. We have to know his voice, and we have to listen to what he says. To not listen ensures that we'll live our spiritual lives wandering aimlessly with uncertainty and fear.

This week we'll learn what it means to listen to God. We'll learn why we should listen to God, and we'll understand the benefits of a life spent listening to his voice.

MOVE

- What voices in your life compete with God's voice?
- Why is it difficult to hear God?
- Why is it important to pay attention to God's voice?

DAY 2

GOD'S WORD

> For he is our God
>> and we are the people of his pasture,
>> the flock under his care.
>> Today, if you hear his voice,
> do not harden your hearts as you did at Meribah,
>> as you did that day at Massah in the desert.

Psalm 95:7–8

"Go to the great city of Nineveh and preach against it, because its wickedness has come up before me."

But Jonah ran away from the Lord and headed for Tarshish. He went down to Joppa, where he found a ship bound for that port. After paying the fare, he went aboard and sailed for Tarshish to flee from the Lord.

Jonah 1:2–3

"Go to the great city of Nineveh and proclaim to it the message I give you."

Jonah obeyed the word of the Lord and went to Nineveh. Now Nineveh was a very important city—a visit required three days.

Jonah 3:2–3

GO

The Old Testament prophets were well known for listening to God. Somehow they knew God's voice so well that they never mistook something else for God's voice, and they never missed the message God was speaking to them.

People don't talk a lot about the Old Testament prophets. Who would? They were weird and did some pretty odd things. Through their strange actions, God's message was clearly proclaimed. What weird things did these men do to tell others what they'd heard God say? Here are my top three favorites:

Amos wandered around preaching doom and gloom. He was called by God, and his message was designed to bring the strayed Israelites back to God. The heart of many of his messages was, "God is coming to destroy you." Not too many people liked what he said.

Hosea listened when God told him to marry a prostitute as a symbol of the religious adultery Israel was committing. When they had children, Hosea gave them names meaning "Not my people" and "Not loved." Hosea's prostitute wife left him, and later he took her back. Not the kind of activity you'd expect from a prophet. However, all of this was at God's direction.

Zechariah heard God's voice and recorded the messianic promises in God's words to him. Today Zechariah is one of the primary Old Testament books we look to for the promise of Jesus the Messiah long before he walked the earth. Certainly, back then not too many people completely understood what Zechariah was saying.

Okay, so your friends aren't lost Israelites. They're not in exile. They're not wandering, disobedient folks. And you're not the kind of person they'd listen to about God. They'll pay attention if you tell them about the new CD you bought or the movie you love. But about God? Probably not.

But you might be wrong. It's quite possible that your friends would listen to you tell them about what you've heard God say. Amos and Hosea and Zechariah might have felt like no one would listen to them.

But, regardless of what they felt about their messages or what God had asked them to do, they obeyed God and did what he asked.

If we're comparing you to the Old Testament prophets, then we've got to compare your friends to the insubordinate, idolatrous Israelites. If the prophets were God's mouthpiece for the Israelites, then you are God's voice for your friends.

Whatever your friends face, you are their prophet. Don't turn the page. Don't lose me here. You are the person God has called to speak to your friends.

You say you're not the outspoken type.

Fine.

You say you don't know what you'll say to them. Confronting them is impossible.

Good.

Yeah, anyone could reach your friends. God could talk to someone else and tell them to talk to your friends. But, chances are, he's not talking to someone else about your friends. He's talking to you about them.

And he's called you to live as a prophet in their face. To do strange things? Maybe. To say strange things? Possibly. But not for the sake of being strange. For the sake of saving your friends. What are you waiting for?

MOVE

- Why is it difficult to be God's voice for your friends?
- What things might God be telling you to say to your friends?
- What would happen if you ignored God's voice?

DAY 3

GOD'S WORD

Consecrate yourselves and be holy, because I am the LORD your God. Keep my decrees and follow them. I am the LORD, who makes you holy.

Leviticus 20:7–8

The LORD appeared to us in the past, saying: "I have loved you with an everlasting love; I have drawn you with loving-kindness.

Jeremiah 31:3

And the words of the LORD are flawless,
    like silver refined in a furnace of clay,
    purified seven times.

Psalm 12:6

GO

You sit in front of a lump of clay. Wet. Brown. Creased and bumpy. You begin hitting and forming it. Wetting your hands over and over. Squeezing and shaping the lump until it slowly becomes something. A sculpture of a horse. A human. After an hour, your lump has become something you're proud of.

Now you have the opportunity to say something to your clay. To your sculpture. What would you say to it? Would you want to tell it how to live? Would you give it directions about how to survive in the world? You sit there, staring at your clay. You pick bits of clay off your hands and roll it between your fingers, thinking about what you want to say to it.

Is that nuts? Why would you speak to clay? Who would?

God did.

Imagine for a moment that you're God. You've created the earth. You've built mountains and carved out oceans. You've created some pretty crazy-looking animals. You've created clouds. Rain. The sun. The moon. Mosquitoes. Imagine too that you've knit together humans. You've built their skeletons, laid veins in their places. Put eyeballs in their sockets. Made brains. Knit hair onto scalps. Twisted bone and skin into fingers. Now imagine that you love this creation. It's your very best work. You're very proud of your work. You love it.

What would you want to say to your creation? Imagine all the things you *could* say to it. You could scold it and tell it all the ways it has disappointed you. You could correct it and make it feel like it will never live up to your dreams. You could pat it on the back, give it a verbal hug, rock it to sleep.

Someone once said that the problem today isn't that God has stopped talking to us. The problem is that we have stopped listening to God. We spend so much time trying to put words in God's mouth that we don't listen to what he says. We're so concerned about using God's Word to prove our point that we don't know what God is saying to us.

You think God isn't talking to you? That's not what's happening. Are you sure you're listening? Are you devoting significant amounts of time sitting in silence, trying to hear his voice? Are you listening to the voice of God speaking through your parents? Your friends? Your youth pastor? Through his Word?

You are God's formed clay. He created your hair. Your fingers. Your eyes. He knows the words you need to hear. His words to you are loving and life changing. As perfectly as you are created, so are God's words for you. He loves you and longs for you to listen for his voice. He can't wait for you to respond.

MOVE

- If you were God, what would you say to you?
- What prevents you from responding to God?
- When have you heard God's voice? What did he say?

DAY 4

GOD'S WORD

Whether you turn to the right or to the left, your ears will hear a voice behind you, saying, "This is the way; walk in it."

Isaiah 30:21

The LORD will guide you always; he will satisfy your needs in a sun-scorched land and will strengthen your frame. You will be like a well-watered garden, like a spring whose waters never fail.

Isaiah 58:11

The watchman opens the gate for him, and the sheep listen to his voice. He calls his own sheep by name and leads them out. When he has brought out all his own, he goes on ahead of them, and his sheep follow him because they know his voice.

John 10:3–4

GO

It's been a good day. School rocked. You nailed the English exam (your weakest subject). Amanda said she'd go out with you this weekend. You didn't argue with your dad during dinner, and you got your homework done way before you went to bed. Good day. Great night. Perfect day.

That night you drift off to sleep feeling like a total success. Satisfied with your abilities and accomplishments. Feeling secure about your life. Warm and cozy. That night the ice storm that had been predicted since Monday finally hit. Not a fierce storm. No snow. No thunder. The rain and the fifteen-degree temperature were enough to stop your small city. The steady twenty-mile-per-hour wind was all it took to freeze tree limbs and power lines. The frozen lines and limbs have snapped through the night.

No power means . . . no heat. No lights. No television. No radio. No computer and Internet. Waking up cold is no fun. Waking up cold and in the dark is even less fun. Lying there freezing in your bed, you open your eyes and realize that the light in the bathroom isn't on, and there's an eerie silence. Even allowing a few minutes for your eyes to adjust doesn't help much. It's too dark to see much of anything.

Relying on your memory, you slowly walk toward the hall. You make your way to your bedroom door, your arms out in front of you. Opening your bedroom door, you can tell something isn't quite right. There's a cold wind blowing through your house. Something smells . . . a combination of rain, wood, and dust. Since you can't see anything, you yell for your parents, whose room is on the opposite side of the house.

"Mom? Dad?"

"Honey, are you all right? Do you have the flashlight? We need the flashlight."

"No, I don't have it. I was hoping you had it."

"Your father thinks he left it by the fridge. Come over to us. Be careful, something's fallen through the roof. The living room is soaked. Can you make it to us? We'll talk you through it. Follow our voices."

You're able to navigate through the house, in the pitch-dark, bypassing the roof and tree that have fallen into your living room. The sound of your parents' voices guide you to them safely.

Often God's voice is like our parents' voices guiding us through a wrecked house. There are times when our lives feel (or really are) smashed. When our lives are wrecked, all we have is God's voice leading us through the rubble. Our only hope is to listen to God, follow his voice, and make our way around dangerous obstacles and toward him.

Is your life a wreck? Can't find your flashlight? Frozen? God is calling to you. It may be dark, but you can trust the voice of the one calling to you, wanting to lead you out of the rubble.

MOVE

- When has obeying God's voice protected you?
- Who does God's voice sound like to you?
- Why should you listen to God's voice?

DAY 5

GOD'S WORD

But Samuel replied: "Does the LORD delight in burnt offerings and sacrifices as much as in obeying the voice of the LORD? To obey is better than sacrifice, and to heed is better than the fat of rams."

1 Samuel 15:22

Hear me, you who know what is right, you people who have my law in your hearts: Do not fear the reproach of men or be terrified by their insults. For the moth will eat them up like a garment; the worm will devour them like wool. But my righteousness will last forever, my salvation through all generations.

Isaiah 51:7–8

He who belongs to God hears what God says. The reason you do not hear is that you do not belong to God.

John 8:47

All this talk about listening to God . . . it's a little too much. As if it weren't enough to try to follow him, avoid sin, and go to church every time the doors are open, now we're adding listening to God to the growing list of Christian responsibilities. It sounds as if somebody *doesn't* want you to follow God, creating all kinds of silly things to weigh you down and prevent you from actually listening.

And maybe we should be asking ourselves, How do we listen to God? Do we have a personal worship service? Are we supposed to pray out loud? Does fasting help? Maybe we should just wait in silence and allow God to speak to us?

The Bible doesn't give us some kind of magic formula for how to hear God's voice. However, it does offer us some examples and ideas we can use to better hear God. Some of these include . . .

Confessing Sin

The Bible is pretty clear about the barrier sin creates. When we're living with sin, we can't hear God. If you can't hear God, maybe it's because sin is creating a barrier. And so, if you think this might be a problem, you need to stop right now and pray, and ask forgiveness for whatever God is reminding you about.

Watchfulness

Sometimes we don't hear God because we're not listening for his voice. When we allow ourselves to be too busy, or when we're not focusing on God's voice, we won't hear him. Have you heard God's voice lately? If you haven't, maybe it's because you're not listening for him.

Knowing His Voice

God's voice can sound like a lot of different people. But knowing God's voice doesn't mean you know what he sounds like; it means that you know when he's talking. See, God can use someone (like a friend or a parent), he can use the Bible, and he can even put thoughts into your head (like when you're praying, or even concentrating on something other than him). God can speak to you in many ways and through many means.

Responding

James 1:22–25 reminds us that when we know the truth and don't do it, we are like people who look at their reflection in a mirror, and once we turn away from the mirror, we forget what we look like. The same is true for responding to God's voice. We have to be listeners *and* doers. We'll talk a little more about doing what God asks a little later in this book.

So often we realize that God is talking, but his voice seems distant. Maybe we're praying about something, and we're eagerly waiting for God to respond. Maybe we're waiting on God for direction, and he seems silent. If you're waiting and not hearing, consider the four things we've talked about. Look for possible sin. Evaluate if you're being watchful. Ask others what God's voice sounds like. And then, when you hear the voice of God, commit to responding and doing what he says.

MOVE

- How can you be more attentive to God's voice?
- What prevents you from responding to God's voice?
- What sin in your life prevents you from hearing God's voice?

DAY 6

GOD'S WORD

A simple man believes anything,
> but a prudent man gives thought to his steps.

Proverbs 14:15

Test everything. Hold on to the good. Avoid every kind of evil.

1 Thessalonians 5:21–22

Dear friends, do not believe every spirit, but test the spirits to see whether they are from God, because many false prophets have gone out into the world. This is how you can recognize the Spirit of God: Every spirit that acknowledges that Jesus Christ has come in the flesh is from God.

1 John 4:1–2

He's the kid in school who's always been a little strange. Larry hangs out with a small group of friends, who are also a little strange. They're the kids who hang out by themselves. They eat together at lunch and sit together at assemblies. They rarely associate with anyone outside their group.

You've always been Larry's friend even though you two don't have a lot in common and even though you're not a part of his small group of friends. The two of you share the same last name, and that means you sit next to each other in classes. Because of this, you've *had* to get to know each other.

Here's what you know about Larry: Even though he's kind of weird, he's got a neat attitude. He's easy to be around, and he's kind of funny. But Larry can be impossible to get to know. Because of his introverted character, it's taken you years to really get to know him. Even though you "know" Larry, you don't usually talk about deep spiritual issues.

In a very rare moment, you and Larry are sitting alone at a lunch table. Absent are Larry's friends and yours. It's just you and Larry, who seems in an unusual mood and begins telling you about his devotions. Larry says that as he was reading his Bible, he heard God tell him that he was supposed to lead your city in saving the homeless people. Larry offers a long story about what he heard God say. You're confused.

"So, Larry," you begin, "how do you know that God has spoken to you?"

"Well, it was a voice I'd never heard. It was in my head, and it sounded like God's voice would sound. And I don't really like homeless people, and I've never really thought about working with them. I think this is what God wants me to do."

"Really? So what are you planning to do?"

Larry tells you all kinds of plans about how he's going to give homeless people money and help build shelters for them. You don't really believe him, but you smile and nod and act like you're really into what he's talking about.

Fast forward to four weeks later. It's been an interesting four weeks.

Just after you and Larry talked, he went missing for four days. You know this because his parents called you asking if you'd seen him, and they told you they hadn't seen Larry in days. They sounded worried. Larry showed up at school one day, and you asked him where he'd been. He told you that he went to live on the streets to experience what it meant to be homeless.

A few days later, you decided to sit with Larry and his friends at lunch. Larry was asking people if he could borrow some money to buy lunch. You asked Larry why he didn't have any money, and he said that he's been giving everything he has to the organizations in your city that help homeless people. Lately Larry looks like he hasn't eaten in days. He smells like he hasn't bathed. He looks like he's been sleeping in a gutter.

You want to talk to Larry, but you're not sure how to do it. How could he know what God's voice really sounds like? Why is Larry reacting so strangely to what he heard God say? You don't want to discourage Larry, but you want to make sure your friend isn't getting into too much danger.

MOVE

- Does God ask us to do things that could harm us?
- What would you say to Larry?
- How do we know for sure that we've heard God's voice?

DAY 7

GOD'S WORD

This day I call heaven and earth as witnesses against you that I have set before you life and death, blessings and curses. Now choose life, so that you and your children may live and that you may love the Lord your God, listen to his voice, and hold fast to him.

Deuteronomy 30:19–20

Jesus answered, "I did tell you, but you do not believe. The miracles I do in my Father's name speak for me, but you do not believe because you are not my sheep. My sheep listen to my voice; I know them, and they follow me. I give them eternal life, and they shall never perish; no one can snatch them out of my hand."

John 10:25–28

As Jesus and his disciples were on their way, he came to a village where a woman named Martha opened her home to him. She had a sister called Mary, who sat at the Lord's feet listening to what he said. But Martha was distracted by all the preparations that had to be made. She came to him and asked, "Lord, don't you care that my sister has left me to do the work by myself? Tell her to help me!"

"Martha, Martha," the Lord answered, "you are worried and upset about many things, but only one thing is needed. Mary has chosen what is better, and it will not be taken away from her."

Luke 10:38–42

GO

There's a great poem by Robert Frost called "The Road Not Taken." It talks about the choices we're confronted with in life and the result of making the choice to take the less popular but more meaningful road of life. Look it up sometime and read the whole poem, but here's the last stanza:

> I shall be saying this with a sigh
> Somewhere ages and ages hence:
> Two roads diverged in a wood, and I—
> I took the one less traveled by,
> And that has made all the difference.*

What message do you think this could send about the choices we make? When people are faced with the choice to listen to God or listen to the world, which might be the more popular or easier choice? Which is the harder choice?

Now take some time to envision two scenarios: (1) one day doing everything you're supposed to do according to what God wants and making all the right, godly choices and (2) one day doing nothing you're supposed to do and making all the wrong, ungodly choices. What was

*Robert Frost, *Mountain Interval* (New York: Henry Holt and Co., 1920; Bartleby.com, 1999), www.bartleby.com/119/, accessed May 13, 2006.

the result at the end of each day? How would living each of those days make you feel at the end of them?

Whether you realize it or not, you choose how you're going to live each day. And how you live each day reveals a couple of other things: your character and what you believe. How you live shows other people (and God) who calls the shots in your life: you or God. Of course, some decisions are made for you, like things your parents want you to do and the stuff you do in school. But things like who you make friends with, how you treat them, and how you choose to reflect God in your relationships and activities—those are some of the things I'm talking about. You can choose to listen to God on how you handle those choices, or you can choose to call your own shots.

Now close your eyes and envision two roads. One leads you with God's direction and his blessings. The other one leads you down a road of self-serving and selfish ambition, which in the end won't help anyone, including yourself. You know which road God wants you to take. Listen to him and take his road, and that will make all the difference in your life.

MOVE

- What have you learned about listening to God from this activity?
- Using what you've learned from this illustration, how would you explain the importance of listening to God to your best friend?
- How can you apply what you've learned and the truth you've discovered from Scripture to your life?

Why Should I Know What I Believe?

DAY 1

GOD'S WORD

"'If you can'?" said Jesus. "Everything is possible for him who believes." Immediately the boy's father exclaimed, "I do believe; help me overcome my unbelief!"

Mark 9:23–24

Then Jesus cried out, "When a man believes in me, he does not believe in me only, but in the one who sent me."

John 12:44

For it is with your heart that you believe and are justified, and it is with your mouth that you confess and are saved.

Romans 10:10

GO

There are some things you just can't flex on. Some rules you can't change.

Take baking a cake, for example. If you change the mixture too much—add too much flour or too much water—you end up with a mess, not a cake. Lower the air pressure in your car tires, and you seriously impede the performance of your car. Your beliefs act and react the same way as altering a recipe or your tire pressure. Add too much of the wrong thing, and you end up with a mess. In danger. On the wrong path.

The most essential thing you can do as a believer is to work out your beliefs. It's essential that you think through *what* you believe about God and *why* you believe it. If you don't think through those things, you run the risk of something contaminating your beliefs without your knowing it. You risk walking a path that goes against every truth in God's Word.

So take a moment right now and do some initial thinking about your beliefs. Write out your top six beliefs about God. These can be things like "God is real" or "Salvation is for everyone." Next to each belief, write why you believe what you wrote.

- _____
- _____
- _____
- _____
- _____
- _____

Was that easy? Were you comfortable trying to explain why you believe those things? Was it easy writing six things you believe about God?

Think about the most basic beliefs every Christian has.

Does God exist?

What's God like?

Is Jesus real?

How do I know the Bible is true?

Trying to understand your beliefs and know why you believe them isn't easy. This week we'll learn more about what we believe, and we'll understand a little better why we believe it.

MOVE

- Why is it important to know what you believe?
- What happens if you're unsure about your beliefs?
- What's the best strategy to better knowing what you believe?

DAY 2

GOD'S WORD

Then you will understand what is right and just
    and fair—every good path.
For wisdom will enter your heart,
    and knowledge will be pleasant to your soul.

Proverbs 2:9–10

Then he continued, "Do not be afraid, Daniel. Since the first day that you set your mind to gain understanding and to humble yourself before your God, your words were heard, and I have come in response to them."

Daniel 10:12

We know that we are children of God, and that the whole world is under the control of the evil one. We know also that the Son of God has come and has given us understanding, so that we may know him who is true. And we are in him who is true—even in his Son Jesus Christ. He is the true God and eternal life.

1 John 5:19–20

GO

Knowing what you believe is like climbing a huge mountain, except you don't know how huge the mountain really is. You can climb and climb and never feel like you're getting anywhere. The more you study, the more you realize there's more to study. The more you learn, the more you realize how much you don't know.

How do you begin the process of knowing and understanding what you believe? How do you go about getting together the information you need to be more informed about your belief in God? Try these:

Read the Bible. Scripture is the starting place for learning about your beliefs. God's Word is the place doctrine and theology flow from. Don't just read your Bible; mark it up. It's not a sin to underline, circle, or write notes in the Bible.

Talk to your parents. If your parents are Christians, they're probably your best second source for knowing what you believe. Ask your parents how they know what they believe. A few simple questions to get them talking might be, Why do you believe in God? and How can you prove that what you believe about Christianity is true?

Surf the Internet. There are tons of places on the Internet that are loaded with facts about Christianity. Consult your parents and youth leader for names of major, reputable organizations. You can also type in "apologetics" or "basic Christian theology" in a search engine. Print out helpful information, and make sure you actually read what you print.

Read books. No doubt the places you surfed on the Net mentioned books that would help you know more about your faith. There are loads of books that will help you know and understand what you believe.

Check out your local Christian bookstore and ask an employee what he or she would recommend.

Talk to your youth pastor. Going to your pastor or youth pastor armed with good questions about your faith is an excellent way to learn more about what you believe. Ask your pastor some key questions like, How can we prove that God exists? How do we know the Bible is true? and How do we know that Jesus is God's Son? Be sure to write down your pastor's answers so you can review them later.

Pray. Because we talk about prayer so much, we often take it for granted and ignore the power it really has. The communication we have with God isn't just there for when we want to complain or when we're sick. We can ask God to help us understand more about him, and we can ask him to help us remember the information we're learning. Today, what will you say to God to help your knowledge of him deepen?

MOVE

- Name one thing you can do today to strengthen your belief.
- Choose one Internet site you can go to this week or one book to read to learn more about what you believe.
- What Scripture passages should you memorize that will help you defend your belief in God?

DAY 3

GOD'S WORD

Preach the Word; be prepared in season and out of season; correct, rebuke and encourage—with great patience and careful instruction. For the time will come when men will not put up with sound doctrine. Instead, to suit their own desires, they will gather around them a great number of teachers to say what their itching ears want to hear.

2 Timothy 4:2–3

Therefore, prepare your minds for action; be self-controlled; set your hope fully on the grace to be given you when Jesus Christ is revealed.

1 Peter 1:13

But in your hearts set apart Christ as Lord. Always be prepared to give an answer to everyone who asks you to give the reason for the hope that you have. But do this with gentleness and respect, keeping a clear conscience, so that those who speak maliciously against your good behavior in Christ may be ashamed of their slander.

1 Peter 3:15–16

GO

It's the day of the big game. This isn't any game—it's *the* game. You've prepared every day after school. You've worked out. Run laps. Lifted weights. Your entire life has been spent preparing for this game. Tonight you'll walk onto the field like a gladiator facing a lion. Shoulder pads. Helmet. Ready for action.

Let's say this scenario is only partly true. Let's say you knew the game was coming but you chose not to prepare. Nights you should have been working out were spent watching television. Meals designed to keep you slim were padded with brownies, soda, chips, and other junk food.

Silly, huh? Would you show up to this game without getting ready? Probably not. To get ready for this game, you'll eat something that will sit well, and you'll probably put on a favorite pair of socks or something—one of those things you put on to ensure that you'll win the game. A "lucky" thing.

Would you show up to the big game without practicing? Certainly not. You know the importance of practice. You know you'll never be good at the sport without constantly perfecting your skills.

Would you show up to the game not trusting the coach enough to listen to him? Would you ignore the coach and his advice for getting better? Of course not. You'd listen to the coach throughout the game. You'd pay attention to his critiques as you worked out and prepared.

Would you show up to the game and ask not to play? Would you be happy to sit on the sidelines and just watch other people score points, make plays, and have people cheer for them? Nah. You'd want to be in the game. You'd want to be there with your friends. You'd want to score points.

That's the exact feeling you should have about knowing what you believe. You shouldn't show up in life without knowing what you believe. You shouldn't live without knowing why you believe what you believe. And sometimes it's important to start small. If you've never thought about some of your foundational beliefs, check out the Scripture passages below.

- Scripture is given by God, and we can trust him not to lie to us (2 Timothy 3:16).
- God is revealed through nature and human conscience (Romans 1:19–23; 2:14–16).
- Humans are created in the image of God (Genesis 1:27).
- Jesus is God (John 1:1–14).
- The Holy Spirit is God (1 Corinthians 2:11; Psalm 139:7).
- Humans are inherently sinful (Genesis 3:1–13; Romans 3:23).
- The remedy for our sin is to confess and accept God's forgiveness (1 John 1:8–9).

How do you begin knowing what you believe? Start with these Scriptures. They'll help you confidently walk onto the field of life.

MOVE

- Why don't many Christians know what they believe?
- What is the most difficult part of researching your beliefs?
- How do you think God feels when we don't know our beliefs?

DAY 4

GOD'S WORD

> I am in pain and distress;
>> may your salvation, O God, protect me.
> I will praise God's name in song
>> and glorify him with thanksgiving.

Psalm 69:29–30

His wife said to him, "Are you still holding on to your integrity? Curse God and die!" He replied, "You are talking like a foolish woman. Shall we accept good from God, and not trouble?" In all this, Job did not sin in what he said.

Job 2:9–10

Dear friends, do not be surprised at the painful trial you are suffering, as though something strange were happening to you. But rejoice that you participate in the sufferings of Christ, so that you may be overjoyed when his glory is revealed. . . . So then, those who suffer according to God's will should commit themselves to their faithful Creator and continue to do good.

1 Peter 4:12–13, 19

GO

When your faith is shaken, what do you do? When you're neck deep in crud, how does that affect your relationship with God? How does facing spiritual attack affect your belief in God?

Remember Job? He was everything. No, you didn't read that wrong. He literally was everything. The Bible notes that he was blameless, right, upright, and well known. He had many kids and lots of livestock. If he lived in modern times, Job would be the kind of man who is looked up to . . . revered . . . loved. He'd be the kind of guy people would beg to run for president but who wouldn't.

Satan convinced God to let him test Job's faithfulness. God allowed it, and Satan slowly took away almost everything Job had. His children died. His animals died. His riches were taken away. And, even though Job cursed his own birth and life, he never cursed God.

Imagine having everything. Can you imagine that? You have every toy, every gadget, every possession you could ever want. And then one day your parents are dead; your kids are dead. Your stuff is taken. Your money disappears.

How would you respond?

How you respond to a situation like that completely exposes what you believe and how strongly you believe it.

Imagine if Job cursed God the moment his kids died. Wouldn't we know what Job believed? Imagine if he cursed God only after the entire testing was over and everything was finally taken. Wouldn't we label Job as the kind of guy who held on till the last moment but in the end gave up and cursed God?

See, we can say anything we want about what we believe. We can profess, proclaim, admit, and even be a light in a dark world. But it's in the serious testings in life that we discover what we *really* believe. It's at the moment when we lose everything that we discover what's really important. And if, in that moment, we've lived for our stuff or our family or our friends, and we've put those things above our relationship with God, we'll discover that what we've trusted in isn't as important as trusting in Christ.

MOVE

- How does Satan confuse us in our belief in God?
- Why does Satan like it when we're not educated in our beliefs?
- Why is it difficult to know what we believe?

DAY 5

GOD'S WORD

So, if you think you are standing firm, be careful that you don't fall! No temptation has seized you except what is common to man. And God is faithful; he will not let you be tempted beyond what you can bear. But when you are tempted, he will also provide a way out so that you can stand up under it.

1 Corinthians 10:12–13

Because he himself suffered when he was tempted, he is able to help those who are being tempted.

Hebrews 2:18

When tempted, no one should say, "God is tempting me." For God cannot be tempted by evil, nor does he tempt anyone; but each one is tempted when, by his own evil desire, he is dragged away and enticed. Then, after desire has conceived, it gives birth to sin; and sin, when it is full-grown, gives birth to death.

James 1:13–15

GO

Knowing what we believe is one thing. But how do we *live* what we believe? Especially in those pretty tough moments? Do your best to figure out how knowing what you believe would influence you in the following situations.

Smoking

Christy, the youth group president, always leads in every situation. She's known for knowing and doing the right thing all the time. Students in the youth group call her regularly to ask for advice and prayer. However, Christy has befriended an unsaved girl at school and has been riding home with her several days each week. Today the girl parked behind a grocery store halfway between school and their home and lit up a joint. Marijuana was a new smell for Christy, and she felt compelled to try it. After sharing the marijuana with her friend, Christy felt guilty and worthless.

How would knowing what she believed have prevented Christy from smoking pot?

In the Car

Laura and Caleb have been dating for three months. Caleb always pushes their relationship physically. When they start kissing, Caleb usually gets a little out of control. Laura has to push Caleb off her, and that makes Caleb pretty frustrated. But lately Laura has been giving in a bit and allowing Caleb to touch her.

How would knowing what he believes help Caleb? How would sticking to her beliefs help Laura?

On the Internet

Mark and Jeff are the typical, ordinary high school guys. Both run cross country and attend youth group regularly. Usually Mark and Jeff hang out after school at Jeff's house. Jeff's dad got an amazingly fast Internet connection last year. Today Jeff started looking around for different sex sites on the Net. When he found one, both guys ogled for many minutes. When they'd seen enough, both guys felt guilty but passed off their feelings and didn't talk about what they'd done.

How would knowing what they believe have helped Mark and Jeff avoid Internet pornography?

MOVE

- How does knowing what you believe help you when you're in a difficult situation?

- Why is it important to stand up for what you believe?
- What prevents you from standing up for your beliefs?

DAY 6

For Ezra had devoted himself to the study and observance of the Law of the LORD, and to teaching its decrees and laws in Israel.

Ezra 7:10

After three days they found him in the temple courts, sitting among the teachers, listening to them and asking them questions. Everyone who heard him was amazed at his understanding and his answers.

Luke 2:46–47

But as for you, continue in what you have learned and have become convinced of, because you know those from whom you learned it, and how from infancy you have known the holy Scriptures, which are able to make you wise for salvation through faith in Christ Jesus. All Scripture is God-breathed and is useful for teaching, rebuking, correcting and training in righteousness, so that the man of God may be thoroughly equipped for every good work.

2 Timothy 3:14–17

GO

Mashir has been a popular kid since you can remember. He's the star of the basketball team, he's in all the school plays, and he's almost a straight-A student. He's extremely popular. Most of the cute, popular girls want to go out with him. All the guys want to be his friend. In fact, you've been Mashir's friend since junior high. Now and then, you and Mashir have had religious discussions, but they usually don't get that deep.

It's a typical day at school, and you and Mashir are sitting with the usual crew at the lunch table. The lunchroom is busy. One of your friends notices that Mashir has a copy of the Qur'an sitting on top of his books. They ask him about it, and that begins an interesting discussion about what kind of stuff is in the Qur'an. Then the conversation takes an interesting turn. Someone asks Mashir where he goes to church. Mashir explains that Muslims don't worship like Christians do.

"That's weird," someone at the table says. "How is that different from Christianity?"

Mashir goes on to explain what he believes about God, Muhammad, righteous living, and several other key ideas. Then he turns to you and asks, "So how is Christianity different from what I believe? What are the differences?" This isn't the first time Mashir has asked you this question, but it's the first time he's asked you in front of other people.

So you begin. Unfortunately, your speech is really short. You're able to explain what you believe about God and Jesus and some other stuff about how you're supposed to go to church. Your explanation is weak, and after that you basically just shut up and hope no one asks questions.

Sam asks a question. Sam always asks questions. He looks at you and asks, "Tell me the difference between what you believe and what Mashir believes. I don't get the difference."

You're paralyzed. Mashir obviously knows what he believes, but you feel like you're caught under a cloud. You look into the faces of Mashir, Sam, and the other kids sitting at the table. Slowly you begin repeating what you just said, trying to say it in another way. Hoping no one was listening the first time.

After a few minutes, Mashir steps in. He explains in a very effective way the differences between Christianity and Islam. His explanation ends with a very challenging statement: "But most smart people think that Christianity is untrue, and, since Islam is more popular, it obviously has the real truth."

Everyone at the table is looking at you. They're waiting to hear what you have to say to Mashir. What will you say?

MOVE

- What would you say to Mashir?
- What can you do to prevent being caught without an answer in a situation like this?
- How does a situation like this affect our witness to our unsaved friends?

GOD'S WORD

But the one who received the seed that fell on good soil is the man who hears the word and understands it. He produces a crop, yielding a hundred, sixty or thirty times what was sown.

Matthew 13:23

Anyone who believes in the Son of God has this testimony in his heart. Anyone who does not believe God has made him out to be a liar, because he has not believed the testimony God has given about his Son. And this is the testimony: God has given us eternal life, and this life is in his Son. He who has the Son has life; he who does not have the Son of God does not have life.

1 John 5:10–12

And the Father who sent me has himself testified concerning me. You have never heard his voice nor seen his form, nor does his word dwell in you, for you do not believe the one he sent. You diligently study the Scriptures because you think that by them you possess eternal life. These are the Scriptures that testify about me, yet you refuse to come to me to have life.

John 5:37–40

GO

What do you *know*? I mean, what's one thing you feel like a complete expert on? Auto racing? Brad Pitt movies? Yodeling? Maybe you already know a lot, or maybe you think there's a lot more for you to know. But chances are, it's something you know a lot about because it's important to you. It's something you care about. It's something you never get tired of. And it feels good to know that you know a lot about it too.

But what I want you to do right now is think of something you really don't know much about. Maybe something like playing the organ, collecting baseball cards, or art. Have you picked something? Now find some time during your day when you'll be with friends or family members and you feel like having a little fun with them. The challenge is this: try to convince these people that you do actually know something about the subject you really know nothing about. Milk it for all it's worth, and do your best to sound persuasive. Can you fool them? (Make sure you tell them you're joking!)

So how far were you able to convince them? Did you have them fooled for a while, or did they find you out right away? How did it feel to try to talk with people about something you knew nothing about? How did not knowing about it affect the way you came across?

As Christians, it's essential that we understand what we believe. That doesn't mean we have to have the answer to every spiritual question. But we definitely need to be real with others who might need some info or advice from us, because it's an opportunity to share God's love with them. So ask yourself this question: *How well do I understand what I believe?* On a scale of one to ten, rate your understanding of your faith (one being hardly understanding at all, and ten being understanding everything you possibly can).

When you talk about something you know about, it feels good. It feels sort of natural. But when you are trying to explain something you don't know much about, it's harder. You might stumble over your words or sound like you're reciting something rather than expressing something from your own mind with your own words.

Don't get me wrong. Even when we deeply understand what we believe, it can still be difficult to share our faith with others. But here's the clincher: even though it's hard, it's way more effective if you know what you're talking about. And when friends come to you with spiritual questions and problems, you'll be able to relate what you believe in a way that makes sense, because it's coming from you and your personal experience.

So dig into your Bible, pray, and get a grip on what you believe. You never know how many lives God can change through you if you're open to his direction and willing to make the most of every opportunity by knowing what you believe.

MOVE

- What have you learned about the importance of knowing what you believe from this activity?
- Using what you've learned from this illustration, how would you explain the importance of knowing what you believe to your best friend?
- How can you apply what you've learned and the truth you've discovered from Scripture to your life?

Why Should I Do What God Asks?

DAY 1

GOD'S WORD

"I will not again make the feet of the Israelites wander from the land I gave their forefathers, if only they will be careful to do everything I commanded them and will keep the whole Law that my servant Moses gave them." But the people did not listen. Manasseh led them astray, so that they did more evil than the nations the LORD had destroyed before the Israelites.

2 Kings 21:8–9

My people are destroyed from lack of knowledge.
Because you have rejected knowledge,
    I also reject you as my priests;
because you have ignored the law of your God,
    I also will ignore your children.

Hosea 4:6

Did the word of God originate with you? Or are you the only people it has reached? If anybody thinks he is a prophet or spiritually gifted, let him acknowledge that what I am writing to you is the Lord's command. If he ignores this, he himself will be ignored. Therefore, my brothers, be eager to prophesy, and do not forbid speaking in tongues. But everything should be done in a fitting and orderly way.

1 Corinthians 14:36–40

GO

Your sister sits in the back of the car. Like she always does. Sitting there making that annoying noise. Like she always does.

Sometimes it would be cool if your parents would just shut her up. Maybe they could duct tape her mouth shut. Maybe they could tie her up and cram her in the trunk. It's not that you don't like her, but your sister has a tendency to be really annoying. That noise gets on your last nerve.

Ever looked at God like you look at your sister? Ever felt that you want to tape God's mouth shut? He's asking too much. Demanding too much. Maybe he's calling you to go on a mission trip or talk to someone about him, and you don't want to do it. Maybe he's asking you to give up something. Maybe he's just asking you to be kind to your little sister.

Week 5   Why Should I Do What God Asks?

Have you ignored God? When? Name four times when you've ignored God on purpose.

- _____
- _____
- _____
- _____

The thing about God asking us to do stuff is it's impossible to get away from him. Sure, we can run. Hide. Disguise ourselves. Ignore what God is asking us to do. But eventually we have to face God. God never gives up, and it's impossible to get away from him.

This week we'll talk about the stuff God wants us to do. We'll talk about how we feel when he interrupts, changes our plans, or asks too much. You can't ignore God. You can't hide. And it's impossible to disguise yourself. So this week let's face what he's asking us to do. Then we'll deal with your annoying sister.

MOVE

- Why do we ignore God's call on our lives?
- Why should we listen to God?
- What things in our lives prevent us from obeying God?

DAY 2

GOD'S WORD

"Go to the great city of Nineveh and preach against it, because its wickedness has come up before me."

But Jonah ran away from the Lord and headed for Tarshish. He went down to Joppa, where he found a ship bound for that port. After paying the fare, he went aboard and sailed for Tarshish to flee from the Lord.

Jonah 1:2–3

"Go to the great city of Nineveh and proclaim to it the message I give you."

Jonah obeyed the word of the Lord and went to Nineveh. Now Nineveh was a very important city—a visit required three days. On the first day, Jonah started into the city. He proclaimed: "Forty more days and Nineveh will be overturned." The Ninevites believed God. They declared a fast, and all of them, from the greatest to the least, put on sackcloth.

Jonah 3:2–5

GO

Jonah was the master of ignoring the obvious call of God. You remember Jonah, don't you? The Old Testament prophet who ran from God's call? The guy who's the perfect example of how to ignore God's call? He's our case study of what happens when you ignore what God asks.

God calls Jonah and asks him to go and warn the people of Nineveh about the judgment of God. Jonah responds with a resounding "No!" That denial of the call of God starts a chain of events that wrecks Jonah's life.

Runs from God.

Caught in a violent storm.

Thrown overboard.

Swallowed by a whale.

Jonah, minding his own business, gets his life interrupted and his plans changed, all because the people of Nineveh need to hear from God. Jonah, Master God ignorer. The guy suffers and suffers big-time, all because he refuses to do what God asked him to do. And he risks the future of the people of Nineveh because he doesn't want to obey God.

Why is he the perfect case study? *What* can we learn about doing what God asks from the life of Jonah? Is it the message, "Obey God or your life will be destroyed!"? Does it mean that God wants obedience and that, if he doesn't get it, he wrecks our lives?

Jonah teaches us that God's plans are perfect. His story demonstrates that God's plan for us is designed to perfectly fit who we are and what we are called to accomplish. Jonah's story also teaches us the opposite of God's plan. You can call it Jonah's plan or even our plan. It's the plan we often create in a last-minute kind of way, when we hear God calling but don't want to obey.

So many times, we think that if we ignore God's call, he'll find someone else to accomplish what he wants. And that might be true. But sometimes God doesn't want to use someone else. He wants to use us. And, if we ignore his call, he'll take us to an uncomfortable place to get our attention, gain our trust, and cause us to obey him.

See, God could take control of you without your permission. He could force you to obey him. However, he chooses not to use that power. Instead, God chooses to *ask* you to obey, and then he hopes you'll follow his call.

MOVE

- When have you lived like Jonah?
- What is God calling you to do?
- What can you do today to obey what God is calling you to do?

DAY 3

GOD'S WORD

"But God did say, 'You must not eat fruit from the tree that is in the middle of the garden, and you must not touch it, or you will die.'" . . . When the woman saw that the fruit of the tree was good for food and pleasing to the eye, and also desirable for gaining wisdom, she took some and ate it. She also gave some to her husband, who was with her, and he ate it.

Genesis 3:3, 6

But as soon as they were at rest, they again did what was evil in your sight. Then you abandoned them to the hand of their enemies so that they ruled over them. And when they cried out to you again, you heard from heaven, and in your compassion you delivered them time after time.

You warned them to return to your law, but they became arrogant and disobeyed your commands. They sinned against your ordinances, by which a man will live if he obeys them. Stubbornly they turned their backs on you, became stiff-necked and refused to listen.

Nehemiah 9:28–29

Consequently, just as the result of one trespass was condemnation for all men, so also the result of one act of righteousness was justification that brings life for all men. For just as through the disobedience of the one man the many were made sinners, so also through the obedience of the one man the many will be made righteous.

Romans 5:18–19

GO

Ask yourself, *How do I know for sure I'm hearing God when I think I hear his voice? How do I know it's him and not my own voice? What kind of double-checking should I do?*

First, make sure you're really hearing God. How can you know? Double-check what you've heard against these ideas:

- God doesn't ask you to sin. He'd never ask you to go against his Word. He wouldn't ask you to do something that would separate you from him.
- God wouldn't ask you to disobey your parents. Unless your parents are abusive, God won't ask you to do anything that breaks the rules they've put into place for you.
- God wouldn't ask you to do something that's against the law. Unless being a Christian is outlawed, God won't ask you to do something that'll get you tossed in jail.
- God might ask you to do something dangerous but not something you're not prepared for.

Next, talk to people you trust about what you're hearing.

- Talk to your parents. Tell them what you've heard. Explain to them how important it is to you that you do what God asks and that you want to be sure about what you're hearing.
- Talk to a trusted friend. A good friend who knows you can be an excellent ally. Explain what you think you've heard from God, and ask your friend to tell you what he or she honestly thinks about it.
- Ask your pastor's opinion. Your pastor probably has an impartial opinion about what's happening in your life. Explain that you want to hear God's voice accurately and that you want to do what you think you hear God saying.

- Tell God what you think you're hearing him say. Explain what you think you've heard, and ask him to confirm it. Spending time in communion and conversation with God is the best way to ensure that you've accurately heard his voice.

MOVE

- Who can you talk to today who will help you understand God's voice?
- What kinds of things is God asking you to do? Witness to your friends? Obey your parents?
- Are there areas in your life where you've ignored God's call? If so, what areas?

DAY 4

GOD'S WORD

The mind of sinful man is death, but the mind controlled by the Spirit is life and peace; the sinful mind is hostile to God. It does not submit to God's law, nor can it do so. Those controlled by the sinful nature cannot please God.

Romans 8:6–8

Humble yourselves, therefore, under God's mighty hand, that he may lift you up in due time. Cast all your anxiety on him because he cares for you.

1 Peter 5:6–7

Submit yourselves, then, to God. Resist the devil, and he will flee from you. . . . Humble yourselves before the Lord, and he will lift you up.

James 4:7, 10

GO

Let's suppose for a moment that God gave you the opportunity to list the things that were difficult for you to surrender to him and the things that were simple for you to surrender to him. Imagine that God has given you this piece of paper to write on to think through the easiest and most difficult areas of surrender for you.

Easy things to surrender:

- _____
- _____
- _____
- _____

Difficult things to surrender:

- _____
- _____
- _____
- _____

Obeying is difficult, huh? Not all the time. If someone told us that we had to eat a pizza, most of us wouldn't have any problem obeying that order, would we? If God told you he'd be giving you a billion dollars, that'd be easy to obey, wouldn't it?

Here's the thing about doing what God asks. Sometimes when God asks us to do something, we feel like we're building small prison camps for ourselves. Like we're being chained to the wall of a sinking ship. Like God is asking us to do something that feels impossible, that will involve us giving our entire lives. Like we'll be led to certain death.

Surrendering ourselves isn't completely like that. When we surrender and do what God asks, it's like we're handing God one string, one area of our lives, and allowing him to control that one string. God holds the end of the string, and when he pulls at it, we move according to the direction he's pulling. Slowly, throughout our lives, we give him more strings. Before long God has complete control. Gradually, God is able to control everything we do. But this doesn't happen all at once; it happens one string at a time.

Does doing what God asks involve obedience? Certainly. Does it involve surrender? Definitely.

When we surrender, we're allowing God to take control and use us. Surrender means never having to have our way. Surrender means giving up that small desire within us that wants to have everything. It means handing God that first string and moving when he tugs it.

What strings haven't you given to God? What parts of you doesn't he control? Giving up that first string is difficult, but it's essential. Today is a great day to give God your first string, don't you think?

- What has been the most difficult thing to obey God about?
- Which thing on your lists above can you surrender today?
- Why is it difficult to surrender things to God?

DAY 5

GOD'S WORD

Teach me knowledge and good judgment,
    for I believe in your commands.
Before I was afflicted I went astray,
    but now I obey your word.

Psalm 119:66–67

You stumble day and night,
    and the prophets stumble with you.
So I will destroy your mother—
    my people are destroyed from lack of knowledge.
Because you have rejected knowledge,
    I also reject you as my priests;
because you have ignored the law of your God,
    I also will ignore your children.

Hosea 4:5–6

For this very reason, make every effort to add to your faith goodness; and to goodness, knowledge; and to knowledge, self-control; and to self-control, perseverance; and to perseverance, godliness. . . . For if you possess these qualities in increasing measure, they will keep you from being ineffective and unproductive in your knowledge of our Lord Jesus Christ.

2 Peter 1:5–6, 8

GO

Ever been eating out with your best friend at a place you love? The food is great. The atmosphere rocks. It's perfect.

And then a baby starts crying.

Across the room, there's a family of five. Everyone at that table is trying to hush a crying two-year-old, but everything they do only makes the angry kid cry more. The dad gives the kid a spoon, and the angry kid throws it back. The mom tries a cracker. The kid chews it and spits it all over the table.

And there you are. You and your best friend. Atmosphere ruined. Food unimportant.

The baby calms down when the server brings the food, but that only lasts a short while. The whole scene gets worse as the father becomes visibly angry with the kid.

"Obey Daddy," the father says as the kid cries louder. "Son, *obey* your father right now."

This only makes the kid angrier. He pulls at the tablecloth enough to dump some of the plates off the table. Drinks spill. Silverware flies. Everyone at the table jumps to avoid getting spilled on. The embarrassed family walks quickly toward the door, carrying the angry, screaming kid along with them.

Have you ever acted like this? I don't mean, have you ever wrecked a table and thrown a fit. I mean, have your parents ever asked you to do something and you totally, completely disobeyed them? Maybe you broke curfew. Maybe it was about going to a party they didn't want you to go to. Maybe it was about schoolwork.

Here's the thing about obeying your parents, and it's almost an exact mathematical equation. The amount of obedience you give your parents is the same amount you'll give God. So, when your parents ask you to do something and you don't do it, chances are pretty good that when God asks you to do something, you'll likely not do it or you'll feel comfortable delaying acting on what God asks.

So often we have a difficult time obeying God because we have our own way of doing things. We have our own agendas. We're like the kid at the table. We want a fork, but our parents will only give us a spoon. We want riches, but God will only give us just enough. We want popularity, but we only get three good, close friends. We love God, but our way is better. It's the way we prefer. It's the way most of us choose.

I think that's why God wants us to listen to him and obey what he asks us to do. Knowledge comes through experience. And experience comes through following God.

- Why should you obey God?
- Why is it difficult to obey him?
- What could God do through you if you always obeyed him?

DAY 6

GOD'S WORD

If you fully obey the LORD your God and carefully follow all his commands I give you today, the LORD your God will set you high above all the nations on earth. . . . The LORD will make you the head, not the tail. If you pay attention to the commands of the LORD your God that I give you this day and carefully follow them, you will always be at the top, never at the bottom.

Deuteronomy 28:1, 13

But Samuel replied: "Does the LORD delight in burnt offerings and sacrifices as much as in obeying the voice of the LORD? To obey is better than sacrifice, and to heed is better than the fat of rams. For rebellion is like the sin of divination, and arrogance like the evil of idolatry. Because you have rejected the word of the LORD, he has rejected you as king."

1 Samuel 15:22–23

For this reason, since the day we heard about you, we have not stopped praying for you and asking God to fill you with the knowledge of his will through all spiritual wisdom and understanding. And we pray this in order that you may live a life worthy of the Lord and may please him in every way: bearing fruit in every good work, growing in the knowledge of God.

Colossians 1:9–10

GO

Bored.

If there's any word that describes how you feel right now, *bored* would be that word. Nothing to do. Sick for the last ten days, you've missed school, practice, and church. At first it was really cool to take the break, and being sick was kind of okay. But now, days into being stuck at home, you're flat bored.

Having missed church two weeks in a row, you're feeling like maybe it's time to get a little spiritual. Have a little church. You flick on the television and turn to the Christian TV station. You've seen this over-dressed, sweaty-faced guy on TV before.

"Friends, God has declared in his Word that, in order to increase your faith, you have to sow a seed in faith to this ministry and watch the Lord Almighty work in your life."

Only boredom could motivate you to watch this. The guy appears out of touch . . . with everything. Weird clothes, funky combed-back hair, and his constant use of the word "friends" pegs this guy as someone who's spent years in freak school.

The prepackaged, carefully produced testimonies begin.

"I was living in a cardboard box. I gave my last dollar to this ministry. I've just purchased my second home. It's a beach house. God is good."

"My wife left me and took the kids too. My drinking was out of control. I was at the end of my rope when I turned on the television and saw your program. Even though I was giving my entire paycheck to support my wife and kids, and even though there wasn't any food in the pantry, I sowed a seed of five thousand dollars. The amount closed my checking account. My wife returned with the kids the very next day. I was able to stop drinking immediately. God has provided everything and has given me my family back as a bonus!"

You begin to wonder how many of these stories are true. You're wondering if God really works like this.

How do you know what God asks you to do? Does he speak through a television evangelist? Does he yell through other people to be heard? And does responding to God mean your life will immediately get better? Your family will get pieced back together? You'll be able to afford three cars, four homes, and vacations in the Bahamas?

Certainly there *are* benefits to doing what God asks. However, those benefits aren't the same for everyone. Some of us might get a lot of money for obeying God, but getting the money shouldn't be our goal. Others of us might get an incredible job or get to travel, but those shouldn't be our goals either. Our goal should be obedience and surrender. Our goal should be to turn over everything in our lives to our Master and allow him to bless us as he sees fit.

- Does obeying God always mean riches and fame?
- Why do people often equate obeying God with giving money?
- How does God feel when we obey him?

DAY 7

GOD'S WORD

Through him and for his name's sake, we received grace and apostleship to call people from among all the Gentiles to the obedience that comes from faith. And you also are among those who are called to belong to Jesus Christ.

Romans 1:5–6

Because of the service by which you have proved yourselves, men will praise God for the obedience that accompanies your confession of the gospel of Christ, and for your generosity in sharing with them and with everyone else.

2 Corinthians 9:13

And this is love: that we walk in obedience to his commands. As you have heard from the beginning, his command is that you walk in love.

2 John 6

GO

Reflections can be found in many places. A mirror, a lake, sometimes a window that's dark on the other side, and even a spoon. But consider where else you can find your reflection. Go around your house and see where else you can see an image or a reminder of yourself.

Look in the mirror. Study your face, the color of your eyes, the shape of your nose. What, or *who*, do you see? Do you see your dad's nose? Your mom's hair? Your grandmother's eyes? Even if you look nothing like your family members, you're still a reflection of them by the way they've influenced your life. And the same way you've been influenced, you also influence others. Maybe it's your siblings, your friends, or the little kids you help out with at church or vacation Bible school. How do you feel about the influence you might be leaving on those people, and can you see the effects of your influence on them?

When you walk through church or school or even down the streets where you live, people will see you, and if they know you, they might say, "That's _____'s kid [or brother or sister or cousin or friend]." You represent a group of people, whether it's your family, your friends, or even your church.

But even with all those reflections we've just discussed, there's still one more. Do you know who else you reflect? It's God. He made each and every one of us in his image. And as a Christian, you are a representative of Christ. Just let that sink in for a moment. How we act, what we say, and what we do are a reflection of Christ in us and influence people's understanding of him.

So what's that got to do with obeying God? Everything. But perhaps the most obvious thing is that when we do obey him and do what he asks us to do, we show his face to others. He uses us as his reflection! When did you first "see" God? Maybe it was a friend who shared the love of Christ with you. Maybe you were influenced by a Sunday school teacher or youth counselor who gave you some extra time and a listening ear. Or maybe it was a miracle or other intervention that only God could design. Those who made the effort to help you see God were reflections of him, simply doing what he asked them to do. And, undoubtedly, that influence has changed your life for eternity.

Your reflection is a pretty big deal. Take some time to take a good look at it and consider how much more powerful it could be, and be open and willing to follow God's direction no matter where it leads.

MOVE

- What have you learned about doing what God asks from this activity?
- Using what you've learned from this illustration, how would you explain to your best friend the importance of obeying God?
- How can you apply what you've learned and the truth you've discovered from Scripture to your life?

Why Should I Care about Persecution?

DAY 1

GOD'S WORD

All your commands are trustworthy;
help me, for men persecute me without cause.

Psalm 119:86

Who shall separate us from the love of Christ? Shall trouble or hardship or persecution or famine or nakedness or danger or sword? As it is written: "For your sake we face death all day long; we are considered as sheep to be slaughtered."

Romans 8:35–36

Persecutions, sufferings—what kinds of things happened to me in Antioch, Iconium and Lystra, the persecutions I endured. Yet the Lord rescued me from all of them. In fact, everyone who wants to live a godly life in Christ Jesus will be persecuted.

2 Timothy 3:11–12

GO

Have you considered the kinds of persecution going on right now around the world?

- In a jail on the other side of the world, there's a man cowering in the corner. Held there because he believes in God, he is unsure if he'll ever be released.
- A woman has been captured, tied to a chair, and beaten repeatedly because she trusts in God instead of a political leader.
- In the middle of an open field, a child lies dead because his parents were caught attending a Christian worship service.
- A young woman is caught reading her Bible by her father, who hates Christians. He beats his daughter repeatedly for her beliefs.
- A young man's parents won't speak to him anymore because of his recent conversion. They've ignored him since he left home for college.

Persecution. Why should you care? Most likely, you've never been beaten; you haven't been ignored, abused, or abandoned because of your faith in Christ. You've never been beaten because you believe in God. You've never been ridiculed because you want to be a virgin when you get married.

You don't have to be beaten or called names to be persecuted. Think for a sec. Write down four ways you can be persecuted without being beaten.

- _____
- _____
- _____
- _____

This week we're talking about persecution. Not about facts and figures or about how many people have been abused for their faith. We'll cover the truth about persecution—how you might be treated poorly because you believe in Christ and how God feels about believers who trust him even when it means they'll get abused.

MOVE

- Why should you care about the persecution of believers in other countries?
- Why do some people find joy in persecuting believers?
- Does God care about persecuted believers? Explain.

DAY 2

GOD'S WORD

If the world hates you, keep in mind that it hated me first. . . . Remember the words I spoke to you: "No servant is greater than his master." If they persecuted me, they will persecute you also. If they obeyed my teaching, they will obey yours also.

John 15:18, 20

. . . so that no one would be unsettled by these trials. You know quite well that we were destined for them. In fact, when we were with you, we kept telling you that we would be persecuted. And it turned out that way, as you well know.

1 Thessalonians 3:3–4

In fact, everyone who wants to live a godly life in Christ Jesus will be persecuted.

2 Timothy 3:12

GO

Let's say you lived when Jesus walked the earth. And after meeting him, you gave up everything you had—your job, your family, your entire life—and followed Jesus. After following him for years, Jesus is captured, persecuted, and killed. How would you handle it if he came back from the dead, hung out, and then disappeared? That kind of adds up to two letdowns, doesn't it? You're enthusiastic when Jesus is alive and then let down when he's gone.

The life of the first disciples must have been tough. Trying to follow in the footsteps of their murdered master couldn't have been easy. Left on their own, the disciples could have chosen one of at least two paths. They could have chosen not to do anything. They could have just rested on the experiences they'd had with Jesus, started a small gathering of believers, and waited.

Their other option (the one they chose) caused them a lot of trouble. They chose to act on what they'd experienced. Maybe it was their experience that compelled them to act. Maybe it was Jesus's commands that motivated them to action. Whatever it was, their acting out Jesus's words set into motion a series of events. As a result, they were persecuted by people who hated Jesus and hated his followers. The apostles' actions moved the people who hated them to act against them.

How were they persecuted?

Foxe's Book of Martyrs gives some incredible accounts about how the disciples died. Thomas (known as the doubter) was shot with a poison dart in India. Peter was crucified upside down. Paul was beheaded. Only John was allowed to live to an old age—he was sent into exile to the island of Patmos.

What a way to go, huh? With the loads of things we can learn from the lives of the apostles, what can we learn from their deaths?

There will always be people who hate Jesus and, as a result, hate you too. Believing in Christ means being instantly hated. But more importantly, believing in Jesus causes action. Faith isn't a sit-on-your-hands kind of thing.

Someone once said that if you believe in Jesus and aren't being persecuted for your belief, then maybe you don't really believe. Belief has obvious results in your life; those results will cause you to be hated. If you're not hated, does that mean you're not living your beliefs? Maybe not. However, sometime in your life you'll be faced with opposition because of your beliefs. Are you ready?

MOVE

- How does the persecution of believers two thousand years ago affect us today?
- Should we expect to be persecuted in the same way as these believers were? Why?
- How does God respond to persecution?

DAY 3

GOD'S WORD

Blessed are those who are persecuted because of righteousness, for theirs is the kingdom of heaven. Blessed are you when people insult you, persecute you and falsely say all kinds of evil against you because of me. Rejoice and be glad, because great is your reward in heaven, for in the same way they persecuted the prophets who were before you.

Matthew 5:10–12

All men will hate you because of me, but he who stands firm to the end will be saved. When you are persecuted in one place, flee to another. I tell you the truth, you will not finish going through the cities of Israel before the Son of Man comes.

Matthew 10:22–23

Blessed are you when men hate you, when they exclude you and insult you and reject your name as evil, because of the Son of Man. Rejoice in that day and leap for joy, because great is your reward in heaven. For that is how their fathers treated the prophets.

Luke 6:22–23

GO

Look, if you've been persecuted, you're not alone. People all over the world are persecuted every day. If you've been beaten, argued with, sidelined, passed over, and ignored because of what you believe, you're not alone. You share in an amazing history of people dating back to the very first believers who trusted in Christ against amazing opposition.

The first followers of Christ were persecuted, although many scholars tell us our understanding of the persecution of these first believers is a little skewed. Many scholars believe that the persecution of the first Christians wasn't widespread and didn't last for decades. Instead, some scholars believe that their persecution lasted only a short time and was in many cases localized, happening in only a few cities.

Whatever the truth is about the persecution of the first believers, it's important to note that they *were* persecuted. Ever stopped to consider why they were persecuted? Here are a few basic reasons.

Their belief in God. These early Christians believed in God, making them targets for people who didn't believe God was real or true. People who believe in God are persecuted simply because they believe he exists.

Their understanding of Jesus. The first believers after the death of Jesus had an understanding of Jesus that made the traditional religious groups frustrated and angry. Traditional Jews didn't believe Jesus was God's Son, and they fought against those who believed Jesus was who he claimed to be.

Their outspoken lives. The result of believing in Jesus meant a change in their lives. They acted differently. They treated each other differently. Their lives were marked by love and selflessness. This amazing impact made many people angry. The first believers' lifestyle was often seen as overly pious, making them targets for those who couldn't stand their humility.

Their willingness to go against the flow. It couldn't have been easy to go against the religious beliefs at the time, but they did. It had to be difficult to stare possible persecution in the face, and yet they still lived what they believed.

These amazing first believers in Jesus set the stage for us today. They're our example for how to live for Christ even when we might be persecuted. So ask yourself the following things:

First, what prevailing beliefs in your life go against your belief in God? Do your parents believe differently than you do? Do the majority of your relatives belong to a completely different religion than you do?

Second, how outspoken is your life? I'm not asking how much you talk about God, although that's part of it. I mean how loud is your life? How much do your actions speak about Christ? If someone were to look at your life (the way you act), would they be able to tell that you believe in God?

Third, how willing are you to go against the flow of belief that surrounds you? Are you willing to risk it and put your life on the line for what you believe? Are you willing to risk your life and live what you believe in another culture? Are you willing to face death because of your love for and belief in God?

MOVE

- Do you have any family members who might persecute you for standing up for your beliefs?
- What things in your life need to change to make it more outspoken?
- How can God help you live a "louder" life?

DAY 4

GOD'S WORD

Do not be afraid of those who kill the body but cannot kill the soul. Rather, be afraid of the One who can destroy both soul and body in hell.

Matthew 10:28

We work hard with our own hands. When we are cursed, we bless; when we are persecuted, we endure it; when we are slandered, we answer kindly. Up to this moment we have become the scum of the earth, the refuse of the world.

1 Corinthians 4:12–13

We are hard pressed on every side, but not crushed; perplexed, but not in despair; persecuted, but not abandoned; struck down, but not destroyed.

2 Corinthians 4:8–9

GO

How much persecution do believers face today? Is persecution real, or is it something people make up to explain why some Christians suffer?

The truth is, Christians all over the world face serious persecution. Believers are beaten, ridiculed, and abused all because they believe in Jesus. Some examples of real-life persecution:

- In China, Christians are required to worship in government-controlled churches. In response to this, evangelical believers have created "house churches" where Christians can practice their faith. The Chinese government arrests and persecutes people caught worshiping in house churches.
- In the Sudan, Christians are the target of Muslim persecution. Christians are sold into slavery for as little as fifteen dollars. Christian mothers are forced to convert to Islam or watch their babies die.
- In Saudi Arabia, police look for Christians to put in prison or behead.
- In Egypt, a group of Muslim extremists have forced thousands of Christians from their homes.

In America we're conveniently separated from violent persecution. Believers aren't forced from their homes. They're not killed. They're not taken into the streets and beaten. They're not forced to watch their kids die. We might face more peaceful forms of persecution—things like legalized abortion or the removal of prayer from school.

Even if we aren't hunted, imprisoned, or jailed, we still face persecution. How do we handle our own persecution and the persecution of people around the world? What proactive steps can we take to guard against being persecuted?

- *Make yourself aware.* There are loads of Internet sites that report on the persecution of believers. Finding these sites is as easy as googling words like "persecution" and "underground church." Search for these places, and read updates on persecution around the world. Pray for the people you read about.
- *Search for subtle persecution.* Persecution can be like spiritual warfare. You don't want to focus all your attention on persecution, and you don't need to always be worried about being persecuted. However, it's important to be aware of the persecution you face (or might face). It's important to be aware of the things that are happening around you that discriminate against your beliefs.
- *Practice patience.* I know it sounds crazy, but being patient and kind when you're being persecuted speaks volumes to the people Satan is using to persecute you. Practice that patience now.

MOVE

- How does being aware of persecution help you face it?
- Why should you be aware of the persecution you face?
- How does having patience help you face persecution?

DAY 5

GOD'S WORD

> Burst into songs of joy together,
>   you ruins of Jerusalem,
> for the Lord has comforted his people,
>   he has redeemed Jerusalem.

Isaiah 52:9

Praise be to the God and Father of our Lord Jesus Christ, the Father of compassion and the God of all comfort, who comforts us in all our troubles, so that we can comfort those in any trouble with the comfort we ourselves have received from God.

For just as the sufferings of Christ flow over into our lives, so also through Christ our comfort overflows. . . . And our hope for you is firm, because we know that just as you share in our sufferings, so also you share in our comfort.

2 Corinthians 1:3–5, 7

GO

Consider the word *comfort* for a moment. What comes to mind?

A pillow and blanket?

A familiar place?

Food?

Your favorite TV show?

When you're living with persecution, your life is anything but comfortable. Your television, soft sheets, good food, or whatever things you find comforting—if you have them—won't touch the miserable feelings you have.

This week you've read about the idea of persecution, and you've read about people in other countries who are experiencing persecution. You've got to ask, what is God's response to all this?

Paul tells us how God responds when we're persecuted. Read 2 Corinthians 1:3–7. He points out that, as we share in the sufferings of Jesus, we also share in the comfort that Jesus experienced. How does Paul explain the comfort of God?

First, Paul points out that God is the God of comfort. God can't stand it when we're being persecuted because of what we believe. He's the God who solves our discomfort with the gift of his comfort. He gives his comfort willingly and without sparing.

Second, Paul explains exactly how God distributes his comfort to us. He uses us. He uses you. When you see a friend who's being picked on because of his or her beliefs, you are God's comfort. In fact, comfort can be a ministry to hurting believers.

Third, God uses our experiences of discomfort to help us comfort others. This is the combination of the first and the second ideas. How do we comfort? What do we say? We know how to comfort, and we know what comforting words to say to others, because we've likely been through those difficult times. Our discomfort leads us to comfort others.

If you're being persecuted, teased, or ridiculed because of what you believe, these words should be comforting. God longs to comfort you. You can expect him to use other believers. So, when a believing friend comes to you offering comfort, recognize it as God's arms and accept the comfort.

If you're not experiencing persecution, God is calling you to be his comforting arms for another believer. His call to you is to go, find a hurting believer, and comfort him or her.

MOVE

- How does God comfort us?
- How does God use believers to comfort hurting believers?
- Why is it important to be available to help hurting believers?

DAY 6

GOD'S WORD

But I tell you: Love your enemies and pray for those who persecute you.

Matthew 5:44

But I tell you who hear me: Love your enemies, do good to those who hate you, bless those who curse you, pray for those who mistreat you.

Luke 6:27–28

Bless those who persecute you; bless and do not curse.

Romans 12:14

GO

Ms. Sanders is notorious around the school for being the teacher who is least sympathetic to Christians. She's never openly antagonistic toward Christians, but she doesn't believe in God, and she doesn't have patience for people who believe that the Bible is true. She's probably one of the most-liked teachers on campus. Her sophomore honors fiction class is often difficult to get into.

So, when Craig mentions that he thinks the Bible was a great piece of literature, Ms. Sanders totally agrees with him but also adds that she doesn't believe it's more than that. Craig counters that he feels it is more than that and believes that the Bible is true and inspired by God.

Even though Ms. Sanders is usually a kind and mild-mannered teacher, Craig's comments touch a nerve in her, and she starts pounding Craig with questions.

"What parts are true?" Ms. Sanders asks snidely.

"I believe all parts of it are true," Craig responds with an air of confidence, just enough to set Ms. Sanders off.

Ms. Sanders comes back with, "Craig, what if God doesn't exist? Have you made any allowance in that brain of yours that God is a being humans made up to make themselves feel better?"

Craig's response: "Believing in God is something you have to have faith about. You can't prove his existence with absolute certainty."

Ms. Sanders's eyes light up. She obviously feels she has the upper hand.

"Ah, faith," Ms. Sanders begins. "The catchall for Christians who can't prove what they believe."

You're sitting in the back of the classroom, watching this whole thing unfold. The room is silent. Everyone is waiting to see what Craig will say that will convince Ms. Sanders that he knows what he's talking about. Craig, who knows you from church, turns around and looks at you, mouthing the words, "Help me out here!"

Craig is relying on you to help him defend his faith. What will you say that will help him and help convince Ms. Sanders that you know why you believe in God?

MOVE

- Why should you stand up with Craig?
- Is it okay to confront a teacher like Ms. Sanders? Explain.
- What could you say or do to help Ms. Sanders really hear about Christ?

GOD'S WORD

Not only so, but we also rejoice in our sufferings, because we know that suffering produces perseverance; perseverance, character; and character, hope. And hope does not disappoint us, because God has poured out his love into our hearts by the Holy Spirit, whom he has given us.

Romans 5:3–5

Therefore, among God's churches we boast about your perseverance and faith in all the persecutions and trials you are enduring.

All this is evidence that God's judgment is right, and as a result you will be counted worthy of the kingdom of God, for which you are suffering. God is just: He will pay back trouble to those who trouble you.

2 Thessalonians 1:4–6

. . . because you know that the testing of your faith develops perseverance.

James 1:3

GO

Freedom is something we all want but often take for granted. It's a part of our everyday lives, and many people have a tendency to assume it will always be there. Like clean air or good health or the future. What does freedom mean to you?

In America we can wear just about anything we want, go just about anywhere we want, and worship God however and whenever we want. But it's not that way in other parts of the world. For other Christians in more distant countries, persecution for what they believe is a regular occurrence. Some even die for their faith.

Can you imagine what it might feel like to be persecuted? Try this experiment. Get a rubber band and put both your hands through it so it's wrapped around your wrists. Keep your hands bound together while you try to complete basic tasks like brushing your teeth, taking out the trash, or making lunch. As you do this, think about how this activity is like being persecuted for what you believe as a Christian. How does this help you get an idea of what it might feel like to be persecuted?

Persecution can happen in America too. Ever known someone who was made fun of or treated badly because of his or her Christian beliefs? Have you ever felt like you were "running against the crowd" in your school because you weren't willing to participate in some activities because they went against what you believe?

You need to care about persecution because, at some point, every Christian is likely to face it. And, even if you're not facing it right now, there are countless other Christians around the world who desperately need your prayers, because they're persecuted every day. They're standing up for Christ when it's really not easy—and sometimes even fatal—for them to do. But they also teach us that the cause of Christ is worth taking a stand for, and they inspire us to take more bold steps in our walk with Christ.

There's no guarantee that we'll live a life without persecution. If we're going to stand up for what we believe, we're going to get some flack for it. So it's better to be ready for it and always place your strength in God's promises for protection and comfort in whatever difficult situations you may face in life.

MOVE

- What have you learned about responding to persecution from this activity?
- Using what you've learned from this illustration, how would you explain to your best friend the importance of caring about persecution?
- How can you apply what you've learned and the truth you've discovered from Scripture to your life?

Why Should I Push Myself?

DAY 1

Do you not know that in a race all the runners run, but only one gets the prize? Run in such a way as to get the prize. Everyone who competes in the games goes into strict training. They do it to get a crown that will not last; but we do it to get a crown that will last forever.

1 Corinthians 9:24–25

Brothers, I do not consider myself yet to have taken hold of it. But one thing I do: Forgetting what is behind and straining toward what is ahead, I press on toward the goal to win the prize for which God has called me heavenward in Christ Jesus.

Philippians 3:13–14

Therefore, since we are surrounded by such a great cloud of witnesses, let us throw off everything that hinders and the sin that so easily entangles, and let us run with perseverance the race marked out for us. Let us fix our eyes on Jesus, the author and perfecter of our faith, who for the joy set before him endured the cross, scorning its shame, and sat down at the right hand of the throne of God. Consider him who endured such opposition from sinful men, so that you will not grow weary and lose heart.

Hebrews 12:1–3

GO

Rounding the corner now. Just one more lap. Seven laps ago, you didn't think you'd make it this far.

Breathe in . . . breathe out . . . you can make it. Just a few hundred more steps.

Your breathing gets more labored. Eyes burning. Chest aching . . .

Half a lap left. Your feet feel like they're made of cement. Your legs feel like tree trunks. Each step takes every ounce of effort you have left.

Push it. If you can just push it, you'll get across the finish line. Keep pushing . . . keep pushing . . .

Crossing the finish line, you collapse. Unable to catch your breath. Unable to walk on your own. You're human Jell-O. Even though you've trained. Even though you've worked out. Even though you're mentally prepared. This has been a lot harder than you thought. Now, lying there, looking up at the clouds and sun, you feel good. Pushing yourself was totally worth it.

What does it take to push yourself? Do you need good training? Need someone standing next to you, telling you to get off your behind? Need to eat right? Exercise regularly? Should you push yourself only in athletics and academics? Do you have to be specially gifted to push yourself?

Truth is, pushing yourself has a lot more to do with desire than ability. Whatever it is, you have to want it and want it bad. Ability? Yeah, ability helps. But sometimes desire is enough. Your will can be enough to help you accomplish whatever it is that God calls you to do.

What do you push yourself to do? What would you love to accomplish that you think is worthy of pushing yourself? List your top three.

- _____
- _____
- _____

This week we're talking about desire, about pushing ourselves. Why should we push ourselves? Should we push ourselves to do only the things God has called us to do? What about pushing ourselves to accomplish something we're passionate about?

This week focus on your desire. Focus on what you know you can accomplish. Focus on what it'll take to get you to accomplish the thing God has called you to do.

MOVE

- What emotional things prevent you from pushing yourself? Fear? Uncertainty?
- What would you be able to accomplish if you pushed yourself this week?
- What could you accomplish for God if you pushed yourself?

DAY 2

And he said: "I tell you the truth, unless you change and become like little children, you will never enter the kingdom of heaven. Therefore, whoever humbles himself like this child is the greatest in the kingdom of heaven."

Matthew 18:3–4

But when the chief priests and the teachers of the law saw the wonderful things he did and the children shouting in the temple area, "Hosanna to the Son of David," they were indignant.

"Do you hear what these children are saying?" they asked him.

"Yes," replied Jesus, "have you never read, "'From the lips of children and infants you have ordained praise'?"

Matthew 21:15–16

Command those who are rich in this present world not to be arrogant nor to put their hope in wealth, which is so uncertain, but to put their hope in God, who richly provides us with everything for our enjoyment.

1 Timothy 6:17

GO

Take a moment and think through your response to these phrases:

"Stretch yourself."
"Be the best."
"Accomplish your dreams."

It's okay to reach for the stars. It's okay to try to make your dreams come true. But, as you're reaching and accomplishing, don't forget to keep your childlike attitude. You're young. Don't forget to play.

Ever watched kids on the playground?

Lindsay stands in the center of the merry-go-round. As it spins, she holds her hands straight up over her head, screaming, "Look at me! Look at me!"

Trevor and Jake are in the fort playing war. They're shooting at each other and pretend fighting. One lobs a rock bomb while the other ducks and hides from pretend shrapnel.

Kelsey is on the swings, legs pumping with determination. She's yelling, "I'm gonna swing so hard I'm going to flip upside down!"

Mark digs a hole deep enough to stand in. He takes one huge scoop after another and eventually gets in, and his legs disappear into the bottom of the hole. "I'm almost in China!" he shouts.

Kids on the playground. They're doing what they do best—playing. What can they teach us about pushing ourselves? Kids are kids, and they don't think about accomplishments and goals and things like that. If you've ever watched children on a playground, you notice that they're not concerned about anything except playing.

What happens when we get older? We forget that we need times to relax and let loose every now and then. We forget to play.

It's easy to push ourselves, isn't it? It's too easy to make ourselves sick trying to accomplish, succeed, and impress. Sometimes we try too hard to get the A. We work too hard to be the best. I'm not saying you shouldn't succeed, and I'm not telling you to be average. Here's what I'm saying.

Remember to play.

Remember that when you were a kid, all you needed was a hole or a rock and a stick. Remember that an autumn afternoon meant going outside and playing in the leaves. Remember that a spring day meant a pickup game of ball with the neighborhood kids. Remember that when you and your best friend from up the street got together, you had the best time. No schedule. No life agenda. No worries and no stress.

MOVE

- How does playing help you understand why you should push yourself?
- What is your favorite way to relax? Why?
- How does playing help you refocus yourself? How does it help you understand God's purpose for you?

DAY 3

And even the very hairs of your head are all numbered. So don't be afraid; you are worth more than many sparrows.

Matthew 10:30–31

We are not like Moses, who would put a veil over his face to keep the Israelites from gazing at it while the radiance was fading away. . . . And we, who with unveiled faces all reflect the Lord's glory, are being transformed into his likeness with ever-increasing glory, which comes from the Lord, who is the Spirit.

2 Corinthians 3:13, 18

Your beauty should not come from outward adornment, such as braided hair and the wearing of gold jewelry and fine clothes. Instead, it should be that of your inner self, the unfading beauty of a gentle and quiet spirit, which is of great worth in God's sight.

1 Peter 3:3–4

GO

People who work in mirror factories have a lot of power. They create sheets of reflective glass that we use to check ourselves out. We use their products to make sure our hair is just right. To make sure we're all tucked in. To see if we've got peanut butter on our cheeks.

Mirrors tell us stories, don't they?

You walk by a mirror and look at yourself. You fix your hair. You straighten your collar. You notice your wrinkles. Mirrors tell us the real story about ourselves.

"My hair is a mess."

"This shirt doesn't fit. It's too tight."

"I'm fat."

"This outfit makes me look hot!"

When we don't like the story the mirror tells us about ourselves, we start to push. We begin thinking our grades aren't good enough. Our looks aren't what they should be. Our lives don't measure up to "perfect." So we push ourselves. We tell ourselves we need to push ourselves to be better, look better, act better.

The mirror tells us a story, and the story isn't always completely true.

But the lie doesn't come from the mirror; the lie comes from ourselves. From our unending desire to be something we're not, or our dissatisfaction with how God made us. This lie is a lot like Satan's first lie, the one he told to Eve in the Garden of Eden. Remember? Satan begins twisting Eve's mind by twisting God's Word, saying, "Did God really say . . . ?" That lie can be translated today: "Did God really say you had any value?" or "Did God say you were any good?" These are the lies that push us toward a perfection we'll never attain. These are the lies that push us away from God and toward whatever ideal Satan can get us to believe.

Our challenge is to redefine, reshape, and recraft our mirrors. We have to decide who we'll listen to.

What do you depend on to tell the real story about you? Who do you listen to for an honest opinion about who you are and what you can accomplish? What do you use to evaluate yourself, your dreams, your character? When we use the wrong set of evaluation questions, we can end up helplessly pushing ourselves.

You know, there are some things that are just true. They're unchanging. One thing that's true and unchanging is that the mirror that tells us we can't or we'll never accomplish anything is a liar. The mirror that tells us we need to push ourselves in order to be happy is a liar. The mirror that tells us we'll be happy only if we accomplish some huge thing is a liar too. When you look at the mirror and it says you're ugly or stupid or not as smart as _____ or not a talented as _____, it's lying. It's distorting the truth—like a funhouse mirror in our minds. The real image is found in what God says about you, how he sees you.

You have to decide what's true about you. You have to decide what's true about your abilities. You have to know yourself, know God's call on your life, and passionately pursue who he made you to be.

MOVE

- What lies have you seen in mirrors?
- In what ways have you attempted to reshape yourself based on a lie?

- How do these "mirror lies" encourage you to push yourself in wrong directions?

DAY 4

Then he said to them all: "If anyone would come after me, he must deny himself and take up his cross daily and follow me. For whoever wants to save his life will lose it, but whoever loses his life for me will save it. What good is it for a man to gain the whole world, and yet lose or forfeit his very self?"

Luke 9:23–25

When Jesus reached the spot, he looked up and said to him, "Zacchaeus, come down immediately. I must stay at your house today." . . . But Zacchaeus stood up and said to the Lord, "Look, Lord! Here and now I give half of my possessions to the poor, and if I have cheated anybody out of anything, I will pay back four times the amount."

Luke 19:5, 8

But whatever was to my profit I now consider loss for the sake of Christ. What is more, I consider everything a loss compared to the surpassing greatness of knowing Christ Jesus my Lord, for whose sake I have lost all things. I consider them rubbish, that I may gain Christ.

Philippians 3:7–8

GO

Do you remember hearing stories about Zacchaeus when you were young? He's the guy who saw Jesus coming and climbed a tree so he could see and hear better.

The Bible isn't kind to Zacchaeus. Scripture describes him as a ladder-climbing pot skimmer. The kind of guy who'd sooner steal your sister's purse than loan you a quarter. The kind of guy who'd look for moments when you're financially strapped and then show up and demand your taxes.

You have to wonder what was going through his mind when he climbed the tree. You have to wonder if he thought he was going to be seen. Could it be that Zacchaeus was competing with Jesus? Imagine it this way. Zacchaeus sees Jesus coming and knows Jesus's message of surrendering all wealth for the poor. Could Zacchaeus have been thinking that the people would be more willing to give up their money to him—maybe if he promised to funnel their money to the poor?

I don't think so. While the Bible seems to portray Zacchaeus as a money-grubbing tax collector, his own actions demonstrate his hunger. I think Zacchaeus climbed the tree to see Jesus because his tax-collecting life hadn't fulfilled him. Imagine: if Zacchaeus had accomplished everything he wanted and was satisfied with what he'd done, he probably wouldn't have climbed the tree that day to see Jesus. Maybe he wouldn't even have gone to see Jesus. He would have gone along with his life and continued taking people's money.

Zacchaeus is a great example for us.

First, he's a clear example of how we shouldn't push ourselves. His example is obvious. Climb the ladder the wrong way, and people will know it. They'll talk bad about what you've achieved and how you achieved it. You'll have enemies. People will hate you. Get accomplishments the Zacchaeus way, and you'll always be looking over your shoulder, watching for the people who are out to get you.

Second, there's no permanent satisfaction in ignoring Jesus. Zacchaeus wouldn't have climbed the tree if he was satisfied with his life. He wouldn't have wanted to hear Jesus if he was happy with his accomplishments. Some might look at Zacchaeus climbing a tree simply as interest in the unique teachings of Jesus. I don't think so. Jesus offered something Zacchaeus had never experienced—satisfaction and fulfillment without cheating and stealing.

Third, it's impossible to ignore spiritual hunger. When you're hungry, you look for food. When you're spiritually lost, you desire someone to come along and teach you truth. Zacchaeus could have climbed up the tree, listened, and then climbed down and gone on his way. But it didn't happen that way. Zacchaeus recognized his hunger and responded. Jesus recognized it too and invited himself over for dinner.

I think the best part about this story is the part we don't know about. What did Jesus say to Zacchaeus at their meal together? What happened to Zacchaeus after the meal? How did Jesus change his life? Did Zacchaeus give back some money like he said he would? Was he ever liked again?

There's no substitute for pushing yourself to know and live for Jesus first. It's okay to pursue other things, but if those things aren't founded on your passionate pursuit of Jesus Christ, you'll just be another Zacchaeus, climbing a tree and craning your neck because you feel totally and completely empty.

MOVE

- In what ways does Zacchaeus's hunger represent yours?
- What things have you allowed in as substitutes in your walk with God?
- How can you get to know Jesus more and invite him into more areas of your life?

DAY 5

GOD'S WORD

Do not those who plot evil go astray?
But those who plan what is good find love and faithfulness.
All hard work brings a profit,
but mere talk leads only to poverty.

Proverbs 14:22–23

Plans fail for lack of counsel,
but with many advisers they succeed.

Proverbs 15:22

There is no wisdom, no insight, no plan
that can succeed against the Lord.

Proverbs 21:30

GO

Ever felt like no matter what you were doing you just could not accomplish anything? You have this great idea, you try and make it happen, and then whatever it was just fizzles out. And then someone comes along and easily accomplishes what you were trying to make happen and they do it with ease.

That's frustrating, huh.

It can be frustrating to watch others accomplish things while we seemingly stand still. It can be frustrating to see others work a little and accomplish a lot while we work hard and get nowhere. We end up being like the student driver in the slow lane while they race past us at warp speed.

How do we move closer to the fast lane? How do we organize ourselves so that we can actually accomplish what we want to—our dreams and goals? Here are some ideas.

Think "Big Dream"

Life direction begins with dreaming up that one big thing that you want to accomplish. Do you have a big dream? Has God laid something on your heart that seems huge, and yet you're convinced that you need to accomplish it? If you have a dream, write it down. Put it someplace where you can see it daily, and be reminded to pray for it and for your ability to accomplish it.

If you don't have a Big Dream yet, don't worry. Take some time to pray and think about a short-term goal. Like for this year or next. Then write it down. It could be a part of finding that Big Dream.

Baby Steps

What's the secret to accomplishing stuff? Break down your idea into smaller goals. In other words, if your goal is to have $500 in six months, break that down into weekly or monthly smaller goals. If your goal is to go to Europe when you're eighteen, break that down too. Think about what you can do each month or each year that will get you ready to make that trip. You might want to write these steps on notebook paper. Then you can keep track of your success.

Who Will Keep You Accountable?

A goal you never tell anyone isn't really a goal; it's more of a private plan. The problem with that kind of plan is that you can easily forget about it or just give up on it. Telling someone about your goal helps make the idea feel important, and it keeps you honest with what you're trying to achieve. Have someone keep asking you about your commitment. Tell him or her to hold you accountable to what you want to achieve.

How Will You Celebrate?

I don't know about you, but the best thing about having big dreams is the act of celebrating those little steps we accomplish when we get a little closer to making that dream happen. So, think to yourself. How will you celebrate what you accomplish? For baby-step goals, you need smaller celebrations. Buying an ice cream cone (or a half-gallon carton). Renting a movie. For bigger dreams, consider celebrating in bigger ways. Going out for an expensive meal or buying yourself a new CD. It's okay to reward yourself for the things you accomplish.

You don't have to be that Podunk driver that other people fly by. You can set the trend, establish a goal, and actually achieve it. All you need is clear thinking, simple steps, and a focused determination to accomplish what you know you were created to do.

MOVE

- What are the top three things you want to accomplish right now with your life?
- What small steps can you take this month to get closer to accomplishing these goals?
- How can you glorify God while you're pursuing your goals?

So then, banish anxiety from your heart
and cast off the troubles of your body,
for youth and vigor are meaningless.

Ecclesiastes 11:10

Be warned, my son, of anything in addition to them. Of making many books
there is no end, and much study wearies the body.
Now all has been heard;
here is the conclusion of the matter:
Fear God and keep his commandments,
for this is the whole duty of man.

Ecclesiastes 12:12–13

In the same way, the Spirit helps us in our weakness. We do not know what we
ought to pray for, but the Spirit himself intercedes for us with groans that words
cannot express. . . . And we know that in all things God works for the good of
those who love him, who have been called according to his purpose.

Romans 8:26, 28

GO

The phone doesn't usually ring this late at night. So when your
mom goes to answer it, she's a little annoyed. You can tell by her body
language that this isn't acceptable. She checks the caller ID and says,
"Sweetheart, you need to be clear with Kendra about this. She's not
supposed to call this late."

"Okay, Mom," you respond, annoyed that Kendra would call so late
but kind of happy that you're getting a break from the homework.

You hear Kendra's sobbing instantly. Kendra has been your best
friend for years. The two of you do everything together. You know each
other's deepest secrets, and you've been through a lot together. Kendra
knows things about you that you'd never share with anyone else. And
you know things about Kendra that she'd never talk about with another
person. You're the only person who knows about her dream to be a
writer. She hasn't told anyone else about her dream of living abroad and

experiencing other cultures. You also know that Kendra pushes herself more than any of your friends. She's extremely focused on her grades, and getting anything other than an A is a personal defeat for her.

Kendra sounds awful. She begins her speech almost before you say "hi."

"Mrs. Herman says there's no way I can get an A in physics," Kendra sobs. "I'm going to blow my GPA. I'm not going to get into the cross-culture program in Europe. I've failed."

"Slow down, chick," you say, trying to understand her and calm her down a bit. "Backtrack a bit."

"You know the physics test last week?"

Yeah, you remembered it. The highest grade in the class was a C, and you failed the test.

"I bombed it. I'm sunk," Kendra continues and starts sobbing loudly.

Kendra's sadness makes you a little frustrated. She never has to study and always gets better grades than you do. When she doesn't get an A on a test or paper, she's upset and openly frustrated. You wish you had her grades, and you wish you cared as much about your grades as she does about hers. You want to help Kendra work through this, but honestly, you wish she'd get a grip and realize that she's not perfect.

"Kendra," you begin, "it's just one exam. You're going to be okay. Your grade will be fine. You'll still be the valedictorian. You're still smart."

In the background, you can hear Kendra talking to her mom. You can't hear the entire conversation, but you can hear a few words. Her mom is upset about the test grade too. You can hear her mom yelling a little, and you can hear Kendra sobbing more and trying to argue back with her mom.

"She's really upset," Kendra says. "I told her about the test and she's angry. She says she's going to call Mrs. Herman tomorrow to talk about my grade, and about how I can work harder in the class."

"I'm sorry, Kendra," you say, trying to sound at least a little sympathetic. "Does it help to know that you're really smart? You know your grades are going to be okay. Just do your best."

"My best?" she says, lowering her voice. "I don't care about doing my best so much as I care about making my mom happy and keeping her off my back. And I'm not smart. I'm scared of what my mom will say or do if I don't get perfect grades."

- How would you help Kendra and her mom talk?
- What could you do to help Kendra with her grades?
- How do our parents affect how we push ourselves?

DAY 7

GOD'S WORD

So we make it our goal to please him, whether we are at home in the body or away from it. For we must all appear before the judgment seat of Christ, that each one may receive what is due him for the things done while in the body, whether good or bad.

2 Corinthians 5:9–10

Are you so foolish? After beginning with the Spirit, are you now trying to attain your goal by human effort? Have you suffered so much for nothing—if it really was for nothing? Does God give you his Spirit and work miracles among you because you observe the law, or because you believe what you heard?

Galatians 3:3–5

We continually remember before our God and Father your work produced by faith, your labor prompted by love, and your endurance inspired by hope in our Lord Jesus Christ.

1 Thessalonians 1:3

GO

We all forget.

Take New Year's resolutions, for example. The week before New Year's, every channel of every network will air something about New Year's resolutions. Or how about graduation? Read stories on the Internet around graduation time. More than likely you'll run across a report somewhere about what graduates plan on doing with their lives.

Why are these reports so fascinating? Sometimes the people who make these goals achieve them and wow the world with how they've accomplished what they set out to do. But more often than not, most people do not achieve what they set in their minds to do.

We forget about the goals we set out to do, and we end up with a long list of "I should haves." The result is regret over the things we never accomplished.

So no pressure here, but think for a moment. If you could decide on three goals for yourself in the coming year, things you personally want to achieve regardless of what everyone else wants you to do, what would those goals be? As you think of them, write each one down on a separate piece of paper. Maybe you'd like to make new friends, have a regular devotion time every day, learn water skiing, or get a B in U.S. history. When you've written down your goals, take a few moments to look them over. Are they doable? Can you really achieve them?

Okay, let's work on motivating yourself to accomplish them. Next, tape each goal to a different object that you use every day. Like your alarm clock or CD player. Maybe take one to school and tape it inside your locker. Be creative. (You could even use a reminder on your cell phone, if you have one, but don't set it to go off in the middle of math class.) Now, think about your week. What can you do to make yourself more aware of each goal so that you consciously work toward it?

Look, making goals is good. And it's important that we remember them and work hard to achieve what we need to achieve. It's all about *perseverance* . . . a really important trait God wants us to develop. He wants to help us rely on him to set the right goals, and then we need to rely on him to help us accomplish our goals—because it shows how strong God is, and it also proves that God can get us through anything we face in life. He wants us to persevere through those challenges and not give up so we can testify to his power and his strength for others to see.

MOVE

- What have you learned from this activity about reminding yourself about your goals?
- Using what you've learned from this illustration, how would you explain the importance of being self-motivated to your best friend?
- Read today's Scriptures again. How can you apply what you've learned to your everyday life?

Why Missions?

Should I Care about

DAY 1

Then I heard the voice of the Lord saying, "Whom shall I send? And who will go for us?"

And I said, "Here am I. Send me!"

Isaiah 6:8

Then he said to his disciples, "The harvest is plentiful but the workers are few. Ask the Lord of the harvest, therefore, to send out workers into his harvest field."

Matthew 9:37–38

Therefore go and make disciples of all nations, baptizing them in the name of the Father and of the Son and of the Holy Spirit, and teaching them to obey everything I have commanded you. And surely I am with you always, to the very end of the age.

Matthew 28:19–20

GO

Sacrifice.

It's the kind of word you really don't want to hear. It ranks right up there with words like *surgery*, *root canal*, and *exercise*. Sacrifice is difficult. We don't run toward it. We don't often like surrendering ourselves.

It's easy to look at missions and say, "I'm not going over to the other side of the world" or "I'm too busy to go to the other side of the tracks to serve at a homeless shelter." We often also think, *Missions is too much of a sacrifice*. And we decide that we won't go.

This is the great tragedy of many missed mission opportunities. We feel unskilled until we learn that the mission field is open to all kinds of opportunities. We feel unprepared, and then we learn that there are people very willing to train us. We feel like we don't have enough money, and then we learn that our church is willing to pay for most of the trip.

The reality of missions is that we don't have to be specially skilled or gifted; we just have to be willing to go. Another reality is that we'd often sooner get a root canal than actually go serve on the mission field.

Can you name some reasons why someone would think the sacrifice of going on a mission trip would be too great? Write three of them below.

- _____
- _____
- _____

This week we're going to work at dispelling our fears and excuses about missions and submitting ourselves to God's desire for us to do missions. We'll learn that the most important aspect of doing missions is the idea of self-sacrifice. And we'll discover that even though it can be difficult to sacrifice ourselves for someone we don't know, it's important and necessary.

MOVE

- Why do you think missions is so important?
- Why do you think missions is so difficult?
- Why is self-sacrifice important in mission work?

DAY 2

GOD'S WORD

He took Peter and the two sons of Zebedee along with him, and he began to be sorrowful and troubled. Then he said to them, "My soul is overwhelmed with sorrow to the point of death. Stay here and keep watch with me." . . . Then he returned to his disciples and found them sleeping. "Could you men not keep watch with me for one hour?" he asked Peter.

Matthew 26:37–38, 40

He told them, "The harvest is plentiful, but the workers are few. Ask the Lord of the harvest, therefore, to send out workers into his harvest field. Go! I am sending you out like lambs among wolves."

Luke 10:2–3

Now an angel of the Lord said to Philip, "Go south to the road—the desert road—that goes down from Jerusalem to Gaza." . . .

Then Philip ran up to the chariot and heard the man reading Isaiah the prophet. "Do you understand what you are reading?" Philip asked.

"How can I," he said, "unless someone explains it to me?" So he invited Philip to come up and sit with him.

Acts 8:26, 30–31

GO

Marty sits on top of the pile of suitcases. He's spent months planning. Months fund-raising. Everyone will be at the airport tomorrow morning. They're expecting to give him the big send-off. This is a moment his entire church has been preparing for—the pastor's sermons aimed at giving money for the trip, the speaking opportunities Marty has had to share his passion, the pictures and questions he's shared in preparation for the trip. Sitting with his suitcases, this almost feels like the end of the journey. What could be more exciting than getting ready to go?

Marty rests himself on top of his suitcases and wonders about his trip. *I wonder if they'll listen. I wonder if they'll even want my help. Am I really sure I'm supposed to do this? Am I convinced that this is where God wants me?*

The next day, Marty climbs aboard a plane headed for Africa, filled with uncertainty, wondering if he'll make an impact, and worried that no one will care that he's left his comfortable life to tell strangers about Jesus.

On the other side of the world, Elon, a young African man, sits by a fire. His daily walks to the river to get water take half the morning. His children run around the thatched-roof house. He's worried that their food supply won't last another week. He needs help, and no one in his village can help him. He wonders if someone will help. He wonders how he'll feed his small family.

Elon stares into the fire and prays. "Send someone to help us, Lord. Move in someone's heart . . . anyone's heart, and bring us someone who will feed us and help us tell others about you."

Are you a Marty—willing to go overseas and help but unsure if anyone wants your help? Right now there's someone on the other side of the world waiting for your gifts and abilities.

Right now God is waiting to use the gifts he's given you for someone in need.

Should you care about missions? Should you care that someone goes overseas or serves locally and helps others?

Yes.

Should you care about *your* doing missions?

Yes. Why? Because God has given you an ability—a talent. He's waiting for you to use it for someone in need. Wouldn't it be a shame if you ignored using your abilities to help someone? Wouldn't it be a shame if you ignored God's call to help those in need? Wouldn't it be a huge loss if God was calling you to witness to someone (either at home or in another country) and you totally ignored God?

MOVE

- What abilities has God given you that you could use on a mission trip?
- Why is ignoring God easier than doing mission work?
- What can you do or learn about to make yourself feel better about doing missions?

DAY 3

GOD'S WORD

While they were worshiping the Lord and fasting, the Holy Spirit said, "Set apart for me Barnabas and Saul for the work to which I have called them." So after they had fasted and prayed, they placed their hands on them and sent them off.

Acts 13:2–3

I do not want you to be unaware, brothers, that I planned many times to come to you (but have been prevented from doing so until now) in order that I might have a harvest among you, just as I have had among the other Gentiles.

Romans 1:13

Don't let anyone look down on you because you are young, but set an example for the believers in speech, in life, in love, in faith and in purity.

1 Timothy 4:12

What does it take to go on a mission trip? Concerned that you don't have what it takes? Worried that you won't do exactly what God wants you to do? Frustrated that you're not entirely clear on all the trip details? Want to know if you're even cut out for this kind of trip?

There are a few things you need to have if you're going on a mission trip. Here are a few.

A Broken Heart

When we're thinking about going to help others, we often struggle with our message. What should we say? How should we serve? God often speaks to us about this, confirming his message in our lives by saying something like, *Before you go and try to help others, I need you to know that without me you're broken and helpless. I'm fixing you. I want to fix the people I'm sending you to.*

We spend a lot of time wondering how to witness to people and worrying if they'll even get what we're trying to communicate. Here's what you need to remember on your next mission trip—a broken heart is your best speech. If you go to someone and give a well-practiced speech, you might help him or her understand God better. However, if you go with a heart that's broken before God, he'll accomplish amazing things.

Ask yourself what breaks your heart. What kind of a help do you want to be for other people?

Abilities

It's easy to doubt that we are skilled to do the work God is calling us to do. What's his message to us? *I made you. I created you. I gave you abilities and skills and passions. I designed you for a work.*

The thing is, a broken heart is essential, but it's not all you need. You've got abilities. Let those guide you as you head into your mission trip. Accept and volunteer for responsibilities that are well within your gifts and passions. Volunteer for jobs you'll excel at. And don't go on a trip doubting your abilities. Here's the thing about God—he's given all of us gifts and abilities. He's given all of us things we can do to build his kingdom. Ask yourself, *What abilities has God given me that I could use on a mission trip?*

Opportunities

How do you miss the opportunities God presents you with to help others? How do you ignore the chances you have to help people understand who God is? Actually, it's easy to miss these opportunities. God's message to us is, *I've called you to help. I'm going to present you with opportunities to do my work at home and possibly in another country. Are you going to notice when I give you chances to help?*

Realizing that we'll be given opportunities, we must be aware. We have to be aware of the people around us who need help. We have to be aware of the best way to tell them the truth about Jesus. Our calling to missions is always combined with opportunities to serve.

A broken heart. Abilities. Opportunities. These aren't the only things you need to do missions. There are also things like willingness, obedience, preparation, and more. Remember, God doesn't just call you, he gives you the gifts and abilities to do the work he calls you to do.

MOVE

- How has your heart been broken? How can you use that for God?
- Why do we sometimes miss God's call to help someone?
- What abilities has God given you that you could use to help others?

DAY 4

But you will receive power when the Holy Spirit comes on you; and you will be my witnesses in Jerusalem, and in all Judea and Samaria, and to the ends of the earth.

Acts 1:8

All the believers were together and had everything in common. Selling their possessions and goods, they gave to anyone as he had need . . . praising God and enjoying the favor of all the people. And the Lord added to their number daily those who were being saved.

Acts 2:44–45, 47

In Damascus there was a disciple named Ananias. The Lord called to him in a vision, "Ananias!"

"Yes, Lord," he answered.

The Lord told him, "Go to the house of Judas on Straight Street and ask for a man from Tarsus named Saul, for he is praying. . . . This man is my chosen instrument to carry my name before the Gentiles and their kings and before the people of Israel."

Acts 9:10–11, 15

GO

You know, people on the other side of the world are starving. They're spiritually hungry. They're needy and wanting and desperate for your help. And, you know, you don't have to go there to know they exist. Television commercials inform you of their needs (right before they toss you a well-crafted sales pitch for helping solve the problem). Pastors speak about the poor and starving on the other side of the world. Are these the only needy people? Do all the saved people live in our country, while the rest of the world is unsaved? Is the point of missions really just a spiritualized overseas trip where you do some good, get some sightseeing in, and then go home?

Here's the thing about mission trips—they're too often really just overly spiritualized vacations. We often want to go to another country to take a cool trip and do a little mission work on the side. We do this to make ourselves feel good and make ourselves appear spiritual.

Look, if you really want to do mission work, if you really want to reach the poor and broken and needy in the world, you don't need to search any farther than your own city. You could make a list of the people in your city who need your help. Here's my list of suggestions, my list of potential opportunities you might look for:

- *The homeless guy picking trash out of the can behind your house.* Can you help feed him?
- *The single mom who's out of work.* She has three cans of soup and half of an old loaf of bread in her cabinet. Her kids are hungry. Can you help feed her kids?
- *The disabled man in your neighborhood.* His yard is a mess, and no one seems to want to help him. Could you give some time to help him with his yard?
- *The teenage mom who attends your school.* She needs someone to watch her kid while she studies for her tests. Could you babysit?
- *Your pastor.* He needs his garage cleaned so his kids can park their bikes inside. Could you help him clean and organize?
- *The girl in your biology class.* She could use someone to pray for her. Do you have a few minutes to pray?

Should you go to the other side of the world? Maybe. There are certainly people there who could use your help. There are organizations that need your help. There are people who need to be fed, who need to be told about Jesus. God just might be calling you to go several thousand miles away and do work there.

And, you know, God might not be calling you to go somewhere else to do mission work. He might be calling you to stay home and serve the people you see every day.

MOVE

- Who in your immediate community could you serve?
- What keeps you from serving these people?
- How could your gifts and abilities help people in your community?

DAY 5

Those who are led by the Spirit of God are sons of God. For you did not receive a spirit that makes you a slave again to fear, but you received the Spirit of sonship. And by him we cry, "*Abba*, Father."

Romans 8:14–15

For this reason I remind you to fan into flame the gift of God, which is in you through the laying on of my hands. For God did not give us a spirit of timidity, but a spirit of power, of love and of self-discipline.

2 Timothy 1:6–7

So we say with confidence, "The Lord is my helper; I will not be afraid. What can man do to me?"

Remember your leaders, who spoke the word of God to you. Consider the outcome of their way of life and imitate their faith.

Hebrews 13:6–7

GO

You know, when we start thinking about missions and witnessing and things like that, Satan begins to work on us. The more we resolve to help others, the more he works to prevent us from working. The more committed we are to go, the more committed he is to keeping us from going. Satan uses any tactic he can to keep us from helping. What kind of lies does Satan speak to keep us from moving when God calls?

"Stay Home"

Here's the message Satan usually speaks: *You don't know the place. You've never been there. You're going to be far away from home, and something tragic might happen to you. You're better and safer at home. Stay home.*

Satan loves to remind us about the great unknown, and he tells us that we should be scared of it. His lie works the comfort angle. If he can make us feel uncomfortable with what we're planning on doing, he just might win. If he can make the potential discomfort feel like a hill that's too huge to climb, he wins. How do you defeat this lie? Educate yourself. Get to know the place you're thinking about going to. Get to know the problems of the area. Get familiar with the people who live there. Get to know their needs. When you do this, you not only educate yourself about how you can help, you take away one of Satan's biggest areas of attack.

"Be Afraid"

Satan's fear-based message usually goes something like this: *If you go on this trip, you're going to die. Okay, maybe you won't die, but people will certainly reject you. They'll try to hurt you. You'll get stranded there, you won't have any fun, you'll be too uncomfortable. Where you're going is too scary. Stay home.*

Satan knows that fear prevents many of us from doing things. And fear is one of his most effective lies too. For example, some people spend their entire lives inside because they're afraid, whether it's fear of being outside, fear of new experiences, or whatever. Fear keeps you from accomplishing what God has called you to do. You know, there's no certain cure to the lying kind of fear Satan tries to infuse into us. Our best defense is to simply trust God. He never calls without providing the power, tools, and protection we need.

"You'll Fail"

Satan's lies about failure strike at the heart of all our fears. His lies usually sound like this: *The people there couldn't care less about you or your message. Go ahead and go; they'll just ignore you. You'll have a great time there talking to yourself, but you're really not skilled enough, and you don't know enough. What good are you? You're going to fail.*

If Satan can get us to feel like a failure, he's won more than just one battle. The feeling of failure seeps into our self-esteem, future goals, and willingness to commit things to God. Satan works this angle either when he's desperate to keep us from going or when he sees that this is his most effective argument. If you already have low self-esteem or already feel worthless, Satan will use that to make you feel more like a failure and, he hopes, prevent you from going.

Here's something you need to remember. Satan will do anything to keep you from going on a mission trip. He'll tell any lie to make you believe you'll never make a difference, you're too stupid, or you don't know enough. This is his job in spiritual warfare, and you are his target.

We have to flee from being ruled by fear, failure, and the unknown. If we're going to care about missions, we have to have the mind of the first disciples, who trusted that Christ would be both their protector and their message. We have to trust that God will guide us, protect us, empower us. We have to believe that our efforts will glorify the one who sent us. We have to trust God more than we trust the lies Satan feeds us. And we have to believe that God's call is stronger than any other negative feeling we have.

MOVE

- What lies have you heard Satan tell you about serving others?
- How have Satan's lies prevented you from serving others?
- What do you think God does to keep us from acting on Satan's lies?

DAY 6

GOD'S WORD

"Now, Lord, consider their threats and enable your servants to speak your word with great boldness. Stretch out your hand to heal and perform miraculous signs and wonders through the name of your holy servant Jesus."

After they prayed, the place where they were meeting was shaken. And they were all filled with the Holy Spirit and spoke the word of God boldly.

Acts 4:29–31

The brothers there had heard that we were coming, and they traveled as far as the Forum of Appius and the Three Taverns to meet us. At the sight of these men Paul thanked God and was encouraged.

Acts 28:15

Let us not become weary in doing good, for at the proper time we will reap a harvest if we do not give up. Therefore, as we have opportunity, let us do good to all people, especially to those who belong to the family of believers.

Galatians 6:9–10

Your pastor gets up at the beginning of the service. Weird, since he doesn't usually get up this early in the worship service. He reaches into his jacket, takes out a letter, and clears his throat into the mic.

"I have a letter," he begins. "It's from Pete, the missionary we've been supporting for three years. You'll remember Pete and his wife have been serving in Africa. I wanted to read Pete's letter instead of paraphrasing it. I hope you'll allow me to get through this. It's a bit long, so settle yourselves and I'll begin reading."

Pastor begins the letter, and it contains the usual greetings to all the people he wants pastor to say hi to for him. The Johnsons and their kids. Pastor's wife (who helped Pete's wife get ready for the birth of their first kid). Mary Smith ("How's it going, Mary? Engaged yet?").

Pastor continues, and, after the hellos, the letter gets serious and melancholy.

"It's been strange here, Pastor. We keep trying to tell people about Jesus, and no one seems to care. Other religions (cults, non-Christian beliefs, etc.) are flourishing. We can't seem to make any headway.

"If not making any headway into the hearts of the people here was our only problem, I think I could handle it. But the other religious leaders here (the ones not from Christian churches) are very antagonistic. They've cast spells on us and the kids. They've openly argued with us in markets, in front of our house, and in worship services. They've made verbal threats against our family. All of this has become more than we can take. We feel defeated, lonely, and scared for our lives. We want to come home."

Pastor looks up from the letter and surveys the congregation. His eyes are wet.

"Folks, this should not happen. I want us to help our friends. What are we going to do?"

Pastor turns and walks to his seat, leaving the podium empty. After a minute of silence with no one moving to speak next, there's a crackle over the sound system. And then a familiar voice flows into the sanctuary.

"Hello, family." Pete's voice sounds like it always has. Apparently, he's sent a tape along with his letter. His tone sounds desperate and uncertain. "We need prayer. Things here are unbearable. The spiritual attacks never end. We're tired. We feel beaten. I'm worried for the kids."

Looking around, you can tell that Pete's words have affected the congregation. People are wiping their eyes. There's genuine concern. Your mind begins to race. You want to do everything. Send money. Pray. Go and help. Tell everyone you know about your hurting missionary friends. You feel helpless to help your friends. You want to help, but you don't know how.

MOVE

- Why do missionaries get discouraged?
- What would you do to help Pete and his family?
- If you walked up to the mic after Pete's tape ended, what would you say to the congregation to motivate them to help Pete?

DAY 7

GOD'S WORD

Again Jesus said, "Peace be with you! As the Father has sent me, I am sending you."

John 20:21

My prayer is not for them alone. I pray also for those who will believe in me through their message, that all of them may be one, Father, just as you are in me and I am in you. May they also be in us so that the world may believe that you have sent me. I have given them the glory that you gave me, that they may be one as we are one: I in them and you in me. May they be brought to complete unity to let the world know that you sent me and have loved them even as you have loved me.

John 17:20–23

How, then, can they call on the one they have not believed in? And how can they believe in the one of whom they have not heard? And how can they hear without someone preaching to them? And how can they preach unless they are sent? As it is written, "How beautiful are the feet of those who bring good news!"

Romans 10:14–15

What image do you see in your mind when you hear the word *missions*? Maybe a faraway country and the faces of exotic-looking people who wear rings in their noses and live in grass huts? Or maybe an urban area, where you see yourself ladling out soup at the homeless shelter or walking the streets with Bibles and tracts under your arm? It's sometimes easier to picture missions going on somewhere far away rather than right where we are. Fact is, missions can happen anywhere. It can happen on the other side of the world, and it can happen right where you live, in your own community. Missions is about spreading the gospel of Jesus Christ, and since that can happen anywhere, missions can happen anywhere.

Find a photo album, and take some time to look through it. You'll probably see family members, friends, teachers, and pets. But your assignment is to look specifically for people who have influenced your spiritual life. As you do, write their names down on a piece of paper. You might find yourself writing down your entire family or a friend or two, and perhaps there isn't even a picture of the person or people you feel have influenced your spiritual life. That's okay. Write their names down anyway.

Now think about how your life might have been different without them. Where would you be now if they hadn't helped you in a spiritual way? God finds a way to reach us somehow and some way. But those on your list have given you a special gift. They cared to be God's instrument in your life, to help you come to know him. *That* is missions.

Next, sit down and write quick notes to a few of those people (or all of them, if you've got the time), thanking them for being God's instrument in your life. Let them know that you see their commitment to Christ, and tell them you're forever changed as a result. Getting a thank-you note from the heart will totally make their day.

Missions is at the core of what we believe as Christians. If we know the eternal change that Christ can make in a person's life, we've just got to tell others about it. Whether you support missions by going to the mission field (the one in your town or the one on the other side of the world), participating in activities at church, giving money, or donating clothes or food to worthy causes, you're showing you care about missions. Find a way to get yourself involved, and you'll be blessed beyond belief—just like you'll bless those who've impacted your life by writing them thank-you notes.

MOVE

- What have you learned about your role in missions from this activity?
- Using what you've learned from this illustration, how would you explain the importance of missions to your best friend?
- How can you apply what you've learned and the truth you've discovered from Scripture to your life?

How Should I Deal with Discouragement?

DAY 1

Then Moses summoned Joshua and said to him in the presence of all Israel, "Be strong and courageous, for you must go with this people into the land that the LORD swore to their forefathers to give them, and you must divide it among them as their inheritance. The LORD himself goes before you and will be with you; he will never leave you nor forsake you. Do not be afraid; do not be discouraged."

Deuteronomy 31:7–8

David also said to Solomon his son, "Be strong and courageous, and do the work. Do not be afraid or discouraged, for the Lord God, my God, is with you. He will not fail you or forsake you until all the work for the service of the temple of the Lord is finished."

1 Chronicles 28:20

But now trouble comes to you, and you are discouraged;
    it strikes you, and you are dismayed.
Should not your piety be your confidence
    and your blameless ways your hope?

Job 4:5–6

GO

Ever seen a train wreck? Know what it takes to derail a huge train? It doesn't take much.

When I was a kid, there was an old tale that you could lay a brick on a railroad track and, when a train came along and hit the brick, the train would derail, causing all kinds of damage and injury. I've never researched whether a small, three-pound brick could wreck a train. Truth is, you'd probably need more than a little brick. You'd need a load of bricks. Honestly, I have no idea how one brick could stop a train.

I think Satan tries to do this with us, though. I imagine he believes that the littlest things do trip us up. He lays things in our paths that he hopes will derail us and prevent us from succeeding in our walk with God. You've got to wonder how Satan knows what will trip us up. How does he know that the things that will trip me won't trip you? How does he know our differences?

The answer lies in Satan's character. I think he knows because he studies us; he looks for our weaknesses. Satan isn't clairvoyant. He can't read our minds and our hearts. He watches and notices where we're weak, and then he uses those weaknesses against us.

Discouragement is one of his favorite weapons. He doesn't discourage each of us in the same way, either. Our best defense is to take a good look at our lives so we can understand in what ways Satan discourages us.

List the three things that discourage you the most. These might be low grades, getting picked on by your older brother, not fitting in at school, or anything else.

- _____
- _____
- _____

When we're discouraged, we lose hope. When we're discouraged, it's easier for us to sin. This week we're going to conquer discouragement.

MOVE

- What makes the things on your list discouragers?
- When we're discouraged, what happens to our relationship with God?
- What weak areas do you think Satan exploits to try to discourage you?

DAY 2

GOD'S WORD

"Be strong and courageous. Do not be afraid or discouraged because of the king of Assyria and the vast army with him, for there is a greater power with us than with him. With him is only the arm of flesh, but with us is the LORD our God to help us and to fight our battles." And the people gained confidence from what Hezekiah the king of Judah said.

2 Chronicles 32:7–8

Hope deferred makes the heart sick,
     but a longing fulfilled is a tree of life.

                         Proverbs 13:12

A bruised reed he will not break,
     and a smoldering wick he will not snuff out.
In faithfulness he will bring forth justice;
     he will not falter or be discouraged
till he establishes justice on earth.
     In his law the islands will put their hope.

                         Isaiah 42:3–4

GO

You've spent hours perfecting your soccer abilities. Your parents have hired special coaches along the way to sharpen your skills. You've bought special pads and gear that leave you with no excuse for failure. Friends have offered pointers. You've joined city leagues and helped lead your team to the city championships. You're proud of yourself too. With not much natural physical ability, you've accomplished a lot.

So when you hear you haven't made the school soccer team, you're beyond angry. You're obviously skilled. You're clearly ready. But the coach says the school has at least a hundred good players. "You're good," he says, "but I need the best. You're not the best—yet. Stick with the city teams another year. When this year's group of seniors graduates, you'll be ready for the team."

You're indignant. You're repulsed by the coach's decision. You're angry that he doesn't see that your talent is clearly better than most athletes in the school. You want to tell him. You want to argue his decision. You want an extra tryout to show him all your skills and all your abilities.

You decide to go to his office and reason with him, but the coach isn't listening. He doesn't want to talk. He doesn't want to see any more of your abilities. He's not interested in hearing anything else from you and encourages you to wait until next year. You leave his office upset and frustrated.

What should you do next? How should you handle your discouragement?

Anger. You could decide to be openly angry at the coach. You could act out, challenge him in public, say really awful things about him to other students. Getting angry at the coach won't help you much, but it'll sure feel good.

Blame. Whose fault is it that you didn't get on the team? The people who trained you? The coach? Maybe it's the fault of the other players in your school who are better than you and maybe better liked by the coach? Maybe it's all your own fault? You could have prepared more. You could have practiced more. Maybe this is all your fault.

Self-doubt. Maybe you're just not good enough. Maybe you're no good at soccer. Maybe you're really not any good at anything. Maybe you should crawl under a rock.

Giving up. Next year is too far away. You've done the city team thing, and that doesn't thrill you. Maybe you should give up, quit playing soccer, and try for something else. Maybe you should put down the soccer ball for the year and pick up the television remote.

What does discouragement do to us? It causes us to doubt ourselves, our ability, our calling. It prevents us from going farther. It prevents us from accomplishing. When we believe we're not good, we give up, get angry, blame, and stop moving. Is this God's plan for us? Does he want us to stop and listen to discouraging lies?

MOVE

- Why is it important to deal with discouragement?
- Why is it easier to give up than to face the thing that discourages you?
- What happens if we get emotional when we're discouraged?

DAY 3

GOD'S WORD

Therefore we do not lose heart. Though outwardly we are wasting away, yet inwardly we are being renewed day by day. For our light and momentary troubles are achieving for us an eternal glory that far outweighs them all. So we fix our eyes not on what is seen, but on what is unseen. For what is seen is temporary, but what is unseen is eternal.

2 Corinthians 4:16–18

Put on the full armor of God so that you can take your stand against the devil's schemes. For our struggle is not against flesh and blood, but against the rulers, against the authorities, against the powers of this dark world and against the spiritual forces of evil in the heavenly realms.

Ephesians 6:11–12

Be self-controlled and alert. Your enemy the devil prowls around like a roaring lion looking for someone to devour. Resist him, standing firm in the faith, because you know that your brothers throughout the world are undergoing the same kind of sufferings.

1 Peter 5:8–9

GO

Here's a quick question.

When was the last time you were really, really discouraged? In that time of discouragement, did you go from a simple letdown all the way to wanting to hide from everyone you know? What effect did your discouragement have on you? Did you give up on yourself? Did you doubt yourself?

When you're feeling discouraged, it's nearly impossible to look at your situation objectively. Think of discouragement as a tool in Satan's hands. Imagine it like this. Satan sees you living your life. He sees your good days, and he doesn't like them. He's sees your bad days, and those he likes. He looks at your life and studies how he can make you have more bad days.

So Satan isn't just the author of discouragement; discouragement is his tool. And he uses this tool whenever and however he can to give us really bad days.

I imagine that Satan uses discouragement like this:

First, he makes you stumble. He causes you to sin. He tempts you. If you give in, it's your fault, but still, he tempted you.

Second, he exploits your mistakes. Have you ever noticed that there are some sins that find their way into public? You get caught. Or you confess in confidence to someone who tells somebody else. Whatever happens, your sin becomes public knowledge. Satan uses that to compound the seriousness of what you've done.

Third, he uses your sin to discourage you. Your discouragement is like putty in his hands. He works to cover you with your own discouragement. He seeks to use your own emotion to drag you down and make you feel like you can't accomplish anything.

Satan doesn't stop there; he uses your discouragement to make you feel worthless. Ever wonder how you can go from experiencing a simple letdown all the way to wanting to live in your closet, or even kill yourself? That's Satan doing what he does best. He's working all the angles and seeking to drag you as low as he can.

How do you handle Satan's discouragement?

First, recognize that he's planning this. Knowledge that he's doing this should be empowering knowledge. Always remember that Satan is working against you.

Second, realize that he's lying. He's not telling the truth. Whatever he's saying, it's not real. When you hear discouraging messages that you're worthless or that what you've done has made an irreparable tear between you and God, that's a lie.

Third, don't react. If you've recognized the source of the discouragement, then you know not to make any stupid decisions.

When you're discouraged, it's okay to find a quiet place where you feel safe. Use this place to hide if you want and insulate yourself from the source of your discouragement. Make the decision not to make any decisions while you're recovering from discouragement.

MOVE

- How does discouragement cause you to stumble in your walk with God?
- What are some ways you can distinguish God's truth from Satan's lies?
- When we decide not to react to our discouragement, what are some of our other options?

DAY 4

So do not throw away your confidence; it will be richly rewarded. You need to persevere so that when you have done the will of God, you will receive what he has promised.

Hebrews 10:35–36

Blessed is the man who perseveres under trial, because when he has stood the test, he will receive the crown of life that God has promised to those who love him.

James 1:12

You have persevered and have endured hardships for my name, and have not grown weary.

Revelation 2:3

GO

In Texas where I live, fire ants are really annoying. I'm not sure if you've ever experienced fire ants, so here's a quick lesson about them.

Fire ants build huge piles of dirt (also known as their homes) in yards. They'll build them everywhere. I'm always amazed at the size and number of the mounds they build. Each summer we have piles everywhere. I don't know a lot about the fire ant, but I think that each of the piles represents a different fire ant community. If that's true, there's a world of fire ants living in our yard during the summer. It's also pretty amazing that these ants can work in the heat we experience during the summer. Our temperature exceeds 100 degrees in midsummer. That makes building a mound hot work.

Each summer we have our fun with the ants, and I'm sure they have their fun with us. I'll mow down their mounds with the lawnmower. And it's a lot of fun knowing I've demolished their homes.

In my own defense, you've got to realize what fire ants do. They destroy lawns. They make big piles of dirt in the yard. They're also sneaky. Fire ants are small, and you don't always notice them. But you can't miss their bite. The bite of the tiny fire ant hurts. It itches. After a few hours, the bite turns into a white puss-filled bump that itches worse than the initial bite. (Personally, this is the only appealing thing about fire ant bites—I love popping the blisters. Is that gross or what?)

Fire ants are a very good example of overcoming discouragement—for a lot of reasons.

Ants don't allow their small size to determine what they can accomplish. Even though there are bigger animals and insects around, the fire ants don't hide. Even though many of the pieces of dirt are large, that doesn't stop them from using those pieces to build their homes. And, even though I continually mow down their mounds, they always build them again. Often in the same spot.

We can look at discouragement the same way. People often try to mow down our mounds. They do it by lying about us or talking about us behind our backs. Or it happens when we realize we're not good at what we thought we were good at. We realize we're not as skilled as we thought. Something really bad happens. Whatever happens, we get discouraged.

Do you feel discouraged? Here's a cool thing to remember—you can rebuild. Use your discouragement to motivate you to rebuild what's been torn down.

MOVE

- Who or what discourages you?
- What's the best way to keep people or circumstances from discouraging you?
- How can you use discouragement to fuel you to accomplish something great?

DAY 5

GOD'S WORD

They had such a sharp disagreement that they parted company. Barnabas took Mark and sailed for Cyprus, but Paul chose Silas and left, commended by the brothers to the grace of the Lord.

Acts 15:39–40

Don't have anything to do with foolish and stupid arguments, because you know they produce quarrels. And the Lord's servant must not quarrel; instead, he must be kind to everyone, able to teach, not resentful.

2 Timothy 2:23–24

But avoid foolish controversies and genealogies and arguments and quarrels about the law, because these are unprofitable and useless.

Titus 3:9

GO

There's nothing more discouraging than a fight. If you've fought with your best friend, you probably know how difficult it is to feel good after a fight with him or her. If you've fought with your parents, you know how rotten you feel. If you've fought with your boyfriend or girlfriend, you realize that a fight can take the wind out of your sails. It can really ruin your perspective on the world.

In Acts 15:36–41 Paul and Barnabas were planning on going on another mission trip. Paul wanted to go back and retrace their previous trip, encouraging and strengthening the people they'd just met. Barnabas wanted to bring John Mark, but John Mark had chickened out on a previous trip, and Paul didn't want to take him. As a result, Barnabas and Paul disagreed. Barnabas headed to Cyprus with John Mark, and Paul took Silas and went back to encourage believers.

Ultimately, the two groups went in different directions with the same purpose. Both groups had a successful ministry, and they eventually got back together. Their disagreement doesn't really seem to be much more than a ripple in the ministry of the formers of early Christian belief and the early church. Does their argument help us understand discouragement? Other than showing us that early believers didn't always get along, do these two guys teach us a valuable lesson?

It had to be discouraging to argue with each other. They must have wondered if they could still tell people about Christ when they didn't get along with each other. Word about their argument probably spread through the early church. Traveling to tell people about God must have felt a little uncomfortable after the fight they just had. It might have been more difficult to explain that God is love after they'd experienced an unloving personal split.

Fighting with someone you love can be a very discouraging thing. We don't know what exactly Paul and Barnabas did to repair their relationship. But, we know the right way to fix a broken relationship. Even if it's awkward or painful or difficult, we need to immediately apologize to our friend, do everything we can to make the relationship right, and then move forward.

Don't let a broken relationship discourage you or your friend. Don't let it keep you from doing something great.

MOVE

- Why is it important to have good relationships with your friends?
- In what way do fights with friends discourage you?
- What is the most difficult aspect of apologizing to a friend you've fought with?

DAY 6

GOD'S WORD

Brothers, think of what you were when you were called. Not many of you were wise by human standards; not many were influential; not many were of noble birth. But God chose the foolish things of the world to shame the wise; God chose the weak things of the world to shame the strong. He chose the lowly things of this world and the despised things—and the things that are not—to nullify the things that are.

1 Corinthians 1:26–28

But he said to me, "My grace is sufficient for you, for my power is made perfect in weakness." Therefore I will boast all the more gladly about my weaknesses, so that Christ's power may rest on me. That is why, for Christ's sake, I delight in weaknesses, in insults, in hardships, in persecutions, in difficulties. For when I am weak, then I am strong.

2 Corinthians 12:9–10

With this in mind, we constantly pray for you, that our God may count you worthy of his calling, and that by his power he may fulfill every good purpose of yours and every act prompted by your faith. We pray this so that the name of our Lord Jesus may be glorified in you, and you in him, according to the grace of our God and the Lord Jesus Christ.

2 Thessalonians 1:11–12

Ray must be made of steel. Really. The guy has taken more hits than anyone you know, and he never stops smiling. He never gets discouraged. Ray wants to be good at something. Unfortunately, he doesn't seem to be good at anything.

For the longest time, Ray wanted to be a singer. He asked you to listen to him sing once, and you weren't impressed. Anyway, Ray went and auditioned for the singing group at your school. After the audition, the music coach told him he needed to pick another group to try out for. Ray asked, "What other music groups are there at our school?" The coach replied, "No, Ray. I mean a totally different group. Try something other than singing. You can't sing."

So Ray opted for the football team. He waited, practiced, and hoped to make the team at the midsemester tryouts. You helped Ray a little, catching the football for him and giving him pointers. Ray tried out, didn't make the team, and seemed kind of discouraged. Trying to feel good at doing something, he went out for baseball, basketball, soccer, and every other team your school has. Ray got rejected from every team.

Now, feeling absolutely depressed, Ray calls you. He's giving up on sports. He's giving up on singing. He just wants to be good at something. The two of you talk for a while, and Ray asks if you'll show him how to change the oil in his car.

You're like, "Ray, oil changes are a long way from sports and singing."

Ray says he wants to be good, really good, at something. Maybe he's no good at sports or singing. Maybe he's better at mechanical stuff. You figure Ray might be right, and you head over to his house (after stopping at the store for oil and a funnel). You pull up, and Ray is waiting on the front porch. He's wearing old jeans and a pair of work gloves.

You and Ray spend time under his car, and you show him all the important stuff he needs to look for. You show him how to remove the seal that holds the oil in. You show him where to pour in the new oil. You show him the whole deal.

At the end, you ask Ray to put the seal back before you pour in the new oil. You go and get the oil while Ray tightens the seal.

"Uh-oh," Ray says. "Is it supposed to be crooked? I've been tightening and tightening, and it won't straighten out."

"Stop!" leaps from your lips as you throw yourself under the car. Ray has put the seal in crooked, and he's stripped the threads. There's no way the seal will go back in without having the threads machined. No way the car will hold any oil until this is done. Ray has ruined his car.

Ray's dad arrives home soon after and learns about the whole ordeal. He yells at you for trying to teach Ray something he clearly doesn't know how to do. He yells at Ray for being so stupid. Ray's dad berates him for five minutes about the mistake he's made.

Later Ray's parents sit him down and explain to him that he'll have to pay for the car repairs. His dad begins yelling at him again and telling him how stupid he is. Ray feels worse and worse. It's bad enough that he feels unskilled at everything; now his dad knows it too and won't stop reminding him about it.

Ray sits on the end of his bed. He's bad at everything. He's let his parents down. Life doesn't feel worth living.

MOVE

- What could you do to help encourage Ray?
- How do our mistakes keep us from accomplishing things?
- What's a healthy way to view the mistakes we make?

DAY 7

GOD'S WORD

In him and through faith in him we may approach God with freedom and confidence. I ask you, therefore, not to be discouraged because of my sufferings for you, which are your glory.

Ephesians 3:12–13

But God, who comforts the downcast, comforted us by the coming of Titus, and not only by his coming but also by the comfort you had given him. He told us about your longing for me, your deep sorrow, your ardent concern for me, so that my joy was greater than ever.

2 Corinthians 7:6–7

> I well remember them,
>   and my soul is downcast within me.
> Yet this I call to mind
>   and therefore I have hope:
> Because of the Lord's great love we are not consumed,
>   for his compassions never fail.
> They are new every morning;
>   great is your faithfulness.

Lamentations 3:20–23

GO

It stinks to be bummed. Is there anything you've felt discouraged about recently? What is it that most often gets you down? Something you can't seem to do right? A relationship that goes bad? Or maybe you're disappointed in yourself . . . your appearance or your performance in school or in a sport? There are lots of different things that can put us down in the dumps.

Let's go back to the age-old test for optimism (or pessimism) to get a better idea of how we should deal with discouragement. Go fill a glass up to the halfway point with your all-time favorite beverage, then step back and take a good look at it. Now ask yourself, *Is the glass half full or half empty?* The theory is that a half-full perspective is optimistic and a half-empty perspective is pessimistic. Yeah, it's a silly test. But, seriously, what's your plan now that you've got that glass of yummy whatever in front of you? Are you going to enjoy it by drinking it slowly, or are you going to gulp it down and then fill the glass to the top with more?

How do you deal with discouragement? Think about some past experiences and reflect on how you were able to get through those times of disappointment and discouragement. Did you talk with someone about your feelings? Write a poem? Read your Bible? Find a distraction like a book or movie or go shoot hoops in your driveway? We've all got our own ways of dealing with our down times. And even when they can't fix our problems, they seem to help us get through them.

But even with all our different ways of coping, we can always rely on one way, which is the best way, and that's to bow our heads in prayer and ask God for support, comfort, and direction. And then trust him to get us through.

Before you're done, search through some of the Bible verses you've read this week and create a motivational or inspirational saying that might help you focus on how best to deal with discouragement. Place the saying where you'll see it a lot, like on your mirror or by your bed, so you'll be reminded often of God's ability to help you through any discouragement you may face.

MOVE

- What have you learned about dealing with discouragement from this activity?
- Using what you've learned from this illustration, how would you explain the importance of facing discouragement to your best friend?
- How can you apply what you've learned and the truth you've discovered from Scripture to your life?

Why Should I Live My Faith in Front of People I Love?

DAY 1

GOD'S WORD

Even though you have ten thousand guardians in Christ, you do not have many fathers, for in Christ Jesus I became your father through the gospel. Therefore I urge you to imitate me.

1 Corinthians 4:15–16

Keep on loving each other as brothers. . . . Remember your leaders, who spoke the word of God to you. Consider the outcome of their way of life and imitate their faith.

Hebrews 13:1, 7

And so you became a model to all the believers in Macedonia and Achaia. The Lord's message rang out from you not only in Macedonia and Achaia—your faith in God has become known everywhere. Therefore we do not need to say anything about it.

1 Thessalonians 1:7–8

GO

Ever play with blankets when you were a kid? Roll your sister up in one and roll her around the living room, even after she begged you to stop? Pull one up around yourself and slide down the stairs? Sometimes when things were slow at home, all you needed was a blanket. Sometimes when you were feeling lost or alone or picked on, pulling a blanket around you made you feel safe, secure, and better.

Living your faith in front of people you love should be like wrapping yourself in a blanket. These people should be safe people who you can live your faith in front of. They should be people who will accept you even if they don't believe like you.

Ready for a difficult question? Is your home a safe place for your faith? Is your home a safe place for your emotions? Is your home a blanket, or is it more like a sheet of wood with nails poking through? Can you live your faith in front of your family? Your closest friends?

Before you can consider *why* you should live your faith in front of people you love, you need to consider *if* you can live your faith in front of them. Can you? What would happen if you took what you believed and made it an active, present part of your daily life? What would happen if you did that in such a way that these people couldn't deny knowing what you believed?

Take a few moments and consider the effect living your faith might have on those closest to you. List a few of those effects below.

- _____
- _____
- _____

Think through that short list above. Is living your faith worth it? Are the effects on those people you love worth it? Is what they might learn from you worth the discomfort you might feel?

You should live your faith in front of people you love because you can influence them. You should do it because they need to see faith lived out. You should do it because they need it. You should do it.

That's what we'll discover this week. How can we live our faith when it feels impossible? How can we do it when people see us at our best and worst?

MOVE

- Is it difficult for you to live what you believe? Why?
- How does living your faith affect people you love?
- Why is it important to live your faith?

DAY 2

I was pushed back and about to fall,
> but the LORD helped me. . . .
I will not die but live,
> and will proclaim what the LORD has done.

Psalm 118:13, 17

A second time they summoned the man who had been blind. "Give glory to God," they said. "We know this man is a sinner."

He replied, "Whether he is a sinner or not, I don't know. One thing I do know. I was blind but now I see!"

John 9:24–25

We proclaim to you what we have seen and heard, so that you also may have fellowship with us. And our fellowship is with the Father and with his Son, Jesus Christ.

1 John 1:3

GO

What do you say to people who know you? How do you communicate what you know about God to the people who have seen you at your best and also at your worst?

First John 1 offers amazing firsthand advice about sharing with others what you know about God. John's explanation is some of the best and often overlooked thinking in the Bible. He assembles a basic explanation of faith in Christ. Here's how he does it.

1 John 1:1–4

¹That which was from the beginning, which we have heard, which we have seen with our eyes, which we have looked at and our hands have touched—this we proclaim concerning the Word of life. ²The life appeared; we have seen it and testify to it, and we proclaim to you the eternal life, which was with the Father and has appeared to us. ³We proclaim to you what we have seen and heard, so that you also may

have fellowship with us. And our fellowship is with the Father and with his Son, Jesus Christ. ⁴We write this to make our joy complete.

John doesn't put together a cool and effective theology based on all kinds of revealed truths. He doesn't assemble a belief based on truths that are scientifically provable. He builds his explanation on experience.

Remember, the New Testament didn't exist when the church was forming in the first century AD. There wasn't any John 3:16 to quote, and early believers didn't have the book of Romans to check their theology against. They did have stories about Christ—stories they shared with each other and passed on from town to town. Some of them wrote their experiences down in letters, but most just told the stories. We often read the Bible like God wrote the words himself. Actually, the Bible was created by God, using humans who wrote about their experiences with him. And the first believers didn't preach sermons to each other (either verbally or in letters); they told each other about their experiences.

1 John 1:5–10

⁵This is the message we have heard from him and declare to you: God is light; in him there is no darkness at all. ⁶If we claim to have fellowship with him yet walk in the darkness, we lie and do not live by the truth. ⁷But if we walk in the light, as he is in the light, we have fellowship with one another, and the blood of Jesus, his Son, purifies us from all sin.

⁸If we claim to be without sin, we deceive ourselves and the truth is not in us. ⁹If we confess our sins, he is faithful and just and will forgive us our sins and purify us from all unrighteousness. ¹⁰If we claim we have not sinned, we make him out to be a liar and his word has no place in our lives.

John continues by saying something like this: "We didn't just experience Christ; we also heard his message. Here is his message: Light has come into the world. This light reveals the sin of humanity." John doesn't just rely on the experience he's had; he relies on the message of Christ.

The message is very simple: God wants a relationship with us. Sin breaks the relationship God wants. John builds this message on the experiences he's had with God. He understands humanity's struggle with obeying God. He understands our fight against our desire to sin.

He knows we long for a relationship with God, yet continue to do things that destroy that relationship.

So you need to stop here and think about how this might translate into your life. I can't tell you how to do that, because I think God applies this message into people's lives differently, but there are general ideas we can apply to our lives.

We have experiences with God that we can share with people we love. These experiences aren't necessarily right or wrong; they're our personal interaction with God. When he reaches into our lives, when he changes us, when he heals or works miracles in us, these are our experiences. These experiences speak louder and better than any pre-packaged explanation we could give about our faith.

These experiences are backed up by the truth Christ shared, and they're backed up by the entire history of the God-humanity relationship. We're estranged from God. We have a broken relationship with our Creator. If we say the relationship isn't broken, we're totally wrong and completely in trouble. God's way out of this brokenness is through surrender.

In your life, you have to find a way to let your actions speak this message. Every action has to tell your family and friends the truth about their need for God and the experiences they can have with him.

MOVE

- How does telling your experience with God help others understand him?
- How do our experiences with God speak louder than our arguments for him?
- How do our actions help prove the validity of our experiences?

DAY 3

GOD'S WORD

Do not cause anyone to stumble, whether Jews, Greeks or the church of God—even as I try to please everybody in every way. For I am not seeking my own good but the good of many, so that they may be saved. Follow my example, as I follow the example of Christ.

1 Corinthians 10:32–11:1

Then Jesus said to his disciples, "If anyone would come after me, he must deny himself and take up his cross and follow me. For whoever wants to save his life will lose it, but whoever loses his life for me will find it."

Matthew 16:24–25

Dear friends, since God so loved us, we also ought to love one another. No one has ever seen God; but if we love one another, God lives in us and his love is made complete in us.

1 John 4:11–12

GO

Who told you about God? How did you learn about Jesus? Who were you around when you first discovered the Holy Spirit? How did you learn the deep truths you now believe? Who taught them to you?

Here's a new phrase we need to talk about. Here you go. Ready? "Person of influence." Kinda big, kinda obscure . . . let's talk about it.

The people who taught you about God, and the people you learned the basics of Christianity from, were people of influence. It might have been a Sunday school teacher or a youth pastor or a good friend or your parents. These people were influencers in your life. They lived the faith; they proclaimed their beliefs with their words and with their lives.

The word *influence* means to live or act in such a way that things are changed. The weather influences whether or not you go outside. Your teachers influence your weekend schedule by giving a lot of homework. Your youth pastor influences your summer by planning a mission trip. There are people and things in your life that influence many of the decisions you make each day. These people don't preface everything they say with, "Now, you know, my job is to influence your decisions and actions. I will now commence influencing you. . . ." They live and act and quietly influence.

Here's a cool thing. You influence too.

Before you completely ignore what I've said, remember that you have a voice. Your actions speak. You know people who listen to you. There are people who watch what you do and imitate you. *You* are a person of influence. Just like people influence you, you influence others.

What does it mean to be a person of influence? There's no passage in the Bible that says, "Ye faithful brethren, here is God's list of rules to being an influential person." Instead, you've got to look at the lives of Bible characters and piece together major teachings from God's Word. What advice about being influential can you glean from God's Word?

Being a person of influence means carrying your cross in all circumstances, at all times. Jesus's death on a cross demonstrates the difficulty of being cross-carrying believers. Being cross carriers means denying ourselves, ignoring what we want for the sake of people we claim to love.

Being a person of influence means loving people unconditionally. First John 4:7–8 is clear about how the people of God are supposed to conduct themselves. We're called to love in all circumstances.

You're influenced. Can you influence? Will you?

MOVE

- How does carrying our cross help prove our message about God?
- Why is loving unconditionally important?
- How can you influence the people around you with your actions?

DAY 4

GOD'S WORD

Therefore let us stop passing judgment on one another. Instead, make up your mind not to put any stumbling block or obstacle in your brother's way. . . . If your brother is distressed because of what you eat, you are no longer acting in love. Do not by your eating destroy your brother for whom Christ died.

Romans 14:13, 15

Be completely humble and gentle; be patient, bearing with one another in love. Make every effort to keep the unity of the Spirit through the bond of peace.

Ephesians 4:2–3

Suppose a brother or sister is without clothes and daily food. If one of you says to him, "Go, I wish you well; keep warm and well fed," but does nothing about his physical needs, what good is it? In the same way, faith by itself, if it is not accompanied by action, is dead.

James 2:15–17

GO

It's not enough to just talk about being a person of influence. It's not enough to just talk about the importance of living your faith in front of people you know. Who should you live your faith in front of? What kind of relationship do you have with them? Here are a few categories:

Your Parents

Your parents have experienced more of life than you have. Whether you want to admit it or not, they know more people, know more about life, and possibly know more about you than you know about yourself. They were there at your birth, they'll be there when you graduate, and they'll be your kids' grandparents. These people who know you so well need a living demonstration of how a Christian should live. You can be an example.

Your Siblings

Like it or not, you influence your siblings. You influence how much time they get in the bathroom. You influence whether or not they'll fight. Have you ever stopped to think about how you can positively influence your siblings? Could you live sacrificially and help them understand sacrifice? Could you allow them to be grumpy one day (without commenting on their grumpiness) and help them understand grace? Could you talk openly about your devotions and influence their understanding of closeness with God?

Your Teachers

Your teachers have difficult lives. They have to be scholars and know their subjects really well. They have to be evaluators and scrutinize your tests and homework. They have to be administrators and effectively manage the class schedule. And they have lives outside school too. They're tired, overworked, and often stressed. Can your faith influence them without your saying anything about your belief in God? Could the way you live help their attitude? Could your life affect their perspective?

Your Friends

Your friends see you more often than anyone else. They know your secrets. They know your rough edges. Your closeness to them can make a difference in their lives. Your beliefs can influence them. Your hugs make a difference. Your honesty makes a difference. Can your positive influence on them help them understand God's love? Could your decisions to live a godly life affect their decisions to live in the footsteps of Christ?

Consider this: what if you made it a point to demonstrate God's love to each of the groups of people above? What would your relationship with your parents be like if you loved them unconditionally? What would your relationship with your siblings be like if you served them unconditionally? What would happen if you did your best to encourage and help your teachers? What if you were real with your friends?

These people know you, and they love you. Your life impacts them in ways you can't imagine. What you do, what you say, and how you live makes a difference in their lives.

MOVE

- How have your parents influenced your belief in God?
- When have your siblings taught you about spiritual things?
- How can you influence and affect the life of a teacher in a positive way?

GOD'S WORD

Therefore, if you are offering your gift at the altar and there remember that your brother has something against you, leave your gift there in front of the altar. First go and be reconciled to your brother; then come and offer your gift.

Matthew 5:23–24

"In your anger do not sin": Do not let the sun go down while you are still angry, and do not give the devil a foothold.

Ephesians 4:26–27

For man's anger does not bring about the righteous life that God desires.

James 1:20

GO

It's been an awful day. Rotten. Miserable. You lost your car keys just after your first class only to find them in the toilet of the guys' bathroom a few hours later. While you were searching for your car keys, you accidentally ran into Sheila, the school hypochondriac. She fell over backward and is claiming you knocked her over on purpose. For that you were called in to see the principal, who didn't believe that it was an accident. To top that off, you failed the science exam.

You've had it. You grab your wet keys and head home. Skipping classes. Forgetting an end-of-the-day literature exam. Skipping soccer practice.

The day has been bad enough to focus all of your anger and frustration on your bedroom door. *Slam.* You hear a bit of a crack too. Not the best sound. Not the kind of sound you really wanted to hear.

It's been bad enough . . . so bad that the slam doesn't begin to make you feel better. You refocus your aggression on your backpack and throw it against your bedroom wall. It dents the wall a little. Enough so you know your parents will notice the dent.

Bad day. Broken door. Hole in the wall. The day isn't getting any better.

You yell a curse word. All of your anger about your day and the door and the wall and your helpless feeling is focused on that one word. You feel guilty—and better. It's not a big deal since no one's home.

"Bad day?" your older brother says, standing in the doorway. The one where your broken door hangs. You didn't realize he was home today.

"Bad day. Leave me alone. Get out."

"Wow. Look at the Christian. You're sooo cool. And you're sooo righteous. Good little Christian kid. Nice to see you, your holiness."

"Get out!" You grab your backpack and throw it at him.

He turns and leaves the room, yelling, "Have a good day, little Jesus," as he walks away.

Your brother's needling makes you angrier. You follow him, screaming more bad words along the way. When you finally get to his room, you're full of rage. The two of you fight, and in the end, you're both a little bloody and very bruised. Your brother isn't done and continues to berate you.

"I thought you were perfect. I thought you didn't sin. I figured you knew all about how to be the good person. Guess I'm better than you, huh?"

You realize what your brother is implying. He's not a believer, but you are. He doesn't know God, but you do. He's simply saying this: You're not allowed to have bad days. If you ever do have a bad day (like today), then you're really not a Christian. You'd love to help your brother understand what it really means to be a Christian, but not right now. Right now you'd rather just attack him some more.

MOVE

- In what ways does having a bad day affect our ability to influence others?
- How does outward anger ruin our ability to live our faith?
- Are there times when it's okay to be angry? When?

GOD'S WORD

Children, obey your parents in the Lord, for this is right. "Honor your father and mother"—which is the first commandment with a promise—"that it may go well with you and that you may enjoy long life on the earth."

Ephesians 6:1–3

Remind the people to be subject to rulers and authorities, to be obedient, to be ready to do whatever is good, to slander no one, to be peaceable and considerate, and to show true humility toward all men.

Titus 3:1–2

Obey your leaders and submit to their authority. They keep watch over you as men who must give an account. Obey them so that their work will be a joy, not a burden, for that would be of no advantage to you.

Hebrews 13:17

GO

Your parents haven't ever really understood your devotion to church. They don't understand why you've rearranged your schedule to make it to early morning discipleship group. They don't get why you want to go on the mission trip. They actually aren't that fond of missions at all. So your wanting to go on the mission trip has caused a huge amount of discussion in the family.

All the preparations have been made at church, and your youth pastor has sent you home with a parents' consent form that will help commit parents to be involved in the preparation for the trip. You need to ask your parents to sign the sheet, so one night after dinner, you talk to your dad about the trip. You already know he doesn't want you to go, and you know he probably won't sign the sheet. He doesn't want anything to do with church, and he certainly won't want to sign the paper.

You begin by showing your dad the sheet and asking him if he'll let you go on the trip.

Your dad begins with, "I'm not sure you should go. You'll be missing work, and you need that money for school. We're really not comfortable with you going to another country either. Your mom and I think you should stay home."

You want to disagree with your dad, but if you do, he'll probably just get mad and refuse even more strongly. And you want to obey your dad too.

"Dad, I really want to do this. I really want to go. I've worked all the fundraisers. I've worked hard to learn more Spanish. I'm really ready to go. Can't I please go?"

Your dad says he'll talk to your mom again, but he's not making any promises.

A few days later, your parents sit you down at the kitchen table to talk about the trip.

"I'm concerned that you'll send a confusing message to the people there," your mom says. She's always been the one most opposed to your going to church.

"The wrong message?" you say, a little sassy.

"The wrong message about God," your dad answers back. "You know people might just think that God is limited to accepting only Christians into heaven. Your mother and I feel that your message would be completely wrong. We'd like you to rethink the purpose of the trip."

You're realizing that your parents are resisting this trip for more than just your safety. Their difference in belief makes it impossible for you to explain the purpose of the mission trip. You're lost about how to explain to them why this trip is so important and why you should go.

MOVE

- How do you live your faith in front of your unbelieving parents?
- How do you tell your unbelieving parents about your beliefs?
- How do you explain things like mission trips to people who aren't Christians?

DAY 7

GOD'S WORD

This is the message we have heard from him and declare to you: God is light; in him there is no darkness at all. If we claim to have fellowship with him yet walk in the darkness, we lie and do not live by the truth. But if we walk in the light, as he is in the light, we have fellowship with one another, and the blood of Jesus, his Son, purifies us from all sin.

1 John 1:5–7

But if anyone obeys his word, God's love is truly made complete in him. This is how we know we are in him: Whoever claims to live in him must walk as Jesus did.

1 John 2:5–6

Dear children, let us not love with words or tongue but with actions and in truth.

1 John 3:18

GO

Gifts are a good thing. If we're getting them, it's exciting and it makes us feel loved. If we're giving them, we feel good because we're making someone else feel good. So, overall, gifts are really very cool.

What's the best gift you ever got from anyone? If you've got it somewhere near you, go get it. If it no longer exists, draw a picture. Or, if you're feeling particularly creative, go make a bunch of mashed potatoes and create a sculpture that looks like your best gift ever.

What made your favorite gift so great? Why does it mean so much to you? Maybe it was the giver. Maybe it was just something you really, really wanted. Or maybe you love it so much because it showed you how much the giver loves you. Have you ever heard that old saying, "It's the thought that counts"? Your gift was probably specially picked for you because it was something you wanted or something that would help or benefit you in some way. But even more important than that, when it was given, the thought was for you and for what you wanted or needed. So the gift isn't so much the object itself but the investment in *you*. No matter what the gift is, it's a gift of love.

So what do gifts have to do with living your faith in front of the people you love? When you live your faith in front of the people you love, you're giving them a gift of love. Your life, lived in a way that directs others to the saving work of Jesus, is an expression of love. It's also a way to pass on the love of Christ to others.

You can show others the love of Christ in so many ways—by making good choices, helping people with their needs through missions, talking with others about the difference Jesus can make, helping with your church's outreach activities, shaking the hand of a visitor at church, giving someone a Bible, standing up for a kid in your school who's made fun of or mistreated . . . and the list goes on and on. If you're searching for ways to make your life a gift to others, you need only to pray, and God will show you.

Jesus's life was a gift to us, and we can in turn make our lives a gift to others. It's a wonderful gift of love. It's the best gift anyone could ever give. It's the opportunity of a lifetime, so don't pass it up.

MOVE

- What have you learned from this activity about living your faith around people you love?
- Using what you've learned from this illustration, how would you explain the importance of being honest about your beliefs to your best friend?
- How can you apply what you've learned and the truth you've discovered from Scripture to your life?

Why Is Boldness So Important?

DAY 1

When I called, you answered me;
you made me bold and stouthearted.

Psalm 138:3

When they saw the courage of Peter and John and realized that they were unschooled, ordinary men, they were astonished and they took note that these men had been with Jesus.

Acts 4:13

Pray also for me, that whenever I open my mouth, words may be given me so that I will fearlessly make known the mystery of the gospel, for which I am an ambassador in chains. Pray that I may declare it fearlessly, as I should.

Ephesians 6:19–20

GO

Standing there with your superman shirt, you're the king, the ruler of your own universe, the master of everything within your sight.

Your cape flaps in the wind. Your teeth gleam in the sunlight. Your hair ripples ever so slightly in the breeze. You're made of stone. Impenetrable. Unconquerable. Unstoppable.

Boldly you approach the ten-armed, sharp-toothed monster with no fear. This isn't a battle of will or brains. This is a battle of muscle. Sheer strength. You'll win. It'll go down. You'll beat it and beat it badly.

You grab the monster by the tentacles and slowly begin to swing it over your head. Round and round, the beast begins to wail as it realizes it's about to get the beating of its life.

And then—"Hey, Superhero! You coming in for dinner?"

You look into the eyes of the beast. Should you kill it now? Or should you let it go? Save it for another day when you need a good hunt? You let it go, looking forward to your next battle.

"Hey, Mr. Caped Wonder. We're all kinda waiting for you in here. Finished yet?"

"Yeah, Dad," you say as you turn to run inside for dinner.

"Here comes our pint-sized rescuer. Save the universe again, kid?"

"I was just about to. What's for dinner?" you say in your superhero voice.

Boldness. Sometimes it doesn't take much . . . just a cape and an imagination. Other times it seems like boldness is an unobtainable emotion or an untouchable concept. No matter how much you try, you just can't be bold about anything. You feel you can't be bold about your relationship with Christ. You think you can't be honest about your salvation with your best friend. You feel like you'd be embarrassed to pray in public.

If you had the power and didn't get discouraged, what five things would you be bold about?

- _____
- _____
- _____
- _____
- _____

This week we're targeting your boldness. Can you be bold when boldness feels impossible? Can you be bold in a room filled with people who believe differently from you?

You can.

MOVE

- What makes being bold so difficult?
- Why is boldness so important?
- How does boldness affect our relationship with Christ?

DAY 2

GOD'S WORD

For two whole years Paul stayed there in his own rented house and welcomed all who came to see him. Boldly and without hindrance he preached the kingdom of God and taught about the Lord Jesus Christ.

Acts 28:30–31

Be on your guard; stand firm in the faith; be men of courage; be strong.

1 Corinthians 16:13

Finally, be strong in the Lord and in his mighty power.

Ephesians 6:10

What if some great thinkers had never thought? What if some gutsy people had never tried? What if they failed and stopped trying? Ever thought of what we *wouldn't* have?

- What if Thomas Edison had never tried? What if he gave up after his numerous failures? We might not have lightbulbs.
- What if Alexander Graham Bell had never tried to communicate cross-country over wires? What if he gave up when he failed? We might not have telephones.
- What if Henry Ford had stopped trying to assemble the automobile? What if he thought his time was worth more than thinking up a crazy invention like that?

What if the next great thinker or inventor or painter or scientist or writer believed the people who told them they'd never amount to anything? What if they looked at their failures and gave up? What would we miss out on? What wouldn't we have?

What if you didn't live boldly for God? What if you never tried? What if you looked at the difficulty and the emotional frustration and said to yourself, "Nah, this is too costly," and you went and did something else? What would the world be missing? Whose life might not be changed?

People in your school might not hear about God. Or maybe they'll hear about God, but they might not hear *your* story. They won't be impacted by your boldness, your story about God. People in your neighborhood might not hear about God. Your parents might miss the message about him.

Do you get the impact your boldness has on your world? Understand how important it is for you to be bold about your relationship with God?

So, really, the question isn't, *Should* you be bold? The question is, When *will* you be bold?

- What things could you accomplish if you tried?
- What things in your life prevent you from being creative and inventive?
- How does endurance help our boldness?

DAY 3

GOD'S WORD

If I speak in the tongues of men and of angels, but have not love, I am only a resounding gong or a clanging cymbal.

1 Corinthians 13:1

Be wise in the way you act toward outsiders; make the most of every opportunity. Let your conversation be always full of grace, seasoned with salt, so that you may know how to answer everyone.

Colossians 4:5–6

But in your hearts set apart Christ as Lord. Always be prepared to give an answer to everyone who asks you to give the reason for the hope that you have. But do this with gentleness and respect.

1 Peter 3:15

GO

Who is the best at being bold? Who is better at pushing and telling and explaining their beliefs without shame? If you look at society, you notice all kinds of people who are openly bold:

- *Telemarketers.* They call and try to tell you about their cool stuff and ideas. They're good at giving one-sided speeches. But their boldness interrupts your dinner.

- *Door-to-door evangelists from that church you've never attended.* They ring and wait for you to answer so they can offer their story about God in their lives. Sometimes, when they hear you're already a Christian, they celebrate. Other times, when they hear of your conversion, they question it and try to convert you to their truth and often not *the* truth. Their boldness can come off as condescending and pious.
- *Salespeople at any store.* Ever shopped for a new car? Ever shopped for a stereo? You're hounded by hawkish salespeople who want you to buy three stereos or a car you could never afford. Their commission-based income makes them ooze with desperation and pushes you out of the store rather than toward the cash register.

There's a negative side of boldness that we often don't talk about. Boldness can become obnoxious. You can be bold to the point of making people angry. In other words, you can use your boldness for God and really make people mad. You can come off like a used car salesman. You can sound like a telemarketer. You can sound more like someone trying to sell something than someone who has a real, life-changing story to tell.

What is the key ingredient in our boldness? How should we be bold?

With love.

In our boldness, we must love. Love-filled boldness means

- speaking the truth with verbal hugs, kind words, and consideration for the other person
- being honest about our relationship with God, telling our story and allowing the Holy Spirit to work on the other person's heart
- looking for people we can serve and love in ways that make a real difference in their lives

Our goal? Be bold without being obnoxious. Be honest without sounding like a salesperson. Be real without being pushy.

Be loving.

Consider Jesus. He lived gently and spoke truthfully. We can too.

- How is loving others being bold?
- How does obnoxious boldness turn people off to Christ?
- How does the Holy Spirit help our boldness?

DAY 4

GOD'S WORD

When his brothers saw that their father loved him more than any of them, they hated him and could not speak a kind word to him. Joseph had a dream, and when he told it to his brothers, they hated him all the more.

Genesis 37:4–5

Now Ahab told Jezebel everything Elijah had done and how he had killed all the prophets with the sword. So Jezebel sent a messenger to Elijah to say, "May the gods deal with me, be it ever so severely, if by this time tomorrow I do not make your life like that of one of them."

1 Kings 19:1–2

The priests and the captain of the temple guard and the Sadducees came up to Peter and John while they were speaking to the people. They were greatly disturbed because the apostles were teaching the people and proclaiming in Jesus the resurrection of the dead. They seized Peter and John, and because it was evening, they put them in jail until the next day. But many who heard the message believed, and the number of men grew to about five thousand.

Acts 4:1–4

GO

Being your father's favorite has its advantages. You get more attention. You get better things. When your siblings have to work hard, you get special treatment.

Joseph was his dad's favorite. Jacob certainly loved his other sons, but there was something special about Joseph. Joseph's dreams were a proclamation of his destiny and a foreshadowing of an amazing series of events all ordained by God. You remember his dreams, right? Actually, it's not his dreams that we're concerned about right now; it's how he told his family about his dreams.

First, he told his dad. Jacob's reaction wasn't that great. Then he told his brothers, who got so mad that they sold him into slavery. Scholars who write books on different biblical events can't agree on Joseph's motives. Was Joseph just happy when he told his brothers about his dreams? Was he just trying to tell them about his amazing experience? Or was Joseph bragging? Was he seeking to demonstrate his superiority over his brothers?

Whatever his motives, Joseph's boldness about his dreams got him in a lot of trouble. The list is kind of depressing.

Tossed into a well.

Sold into slavery.

Lied about.

Thrown in prison.

If you knew being bold was going to cause you this much trouble, would you take the risk? Could you be bold if you knew the result of your boldness was a long trip down a well? Would you be bold if you knew the result would be people lying about you? Does slavery sound fun? Does jail sound like a cool result of your boldness?

The story of Joseph points out both the need for boldness and the result of that boldness. Through Joseph's boldness, thousands of Egyptians were saved from starving during a seven-year famine.

Joseph's boldness was the result of a convincing dream where God clearly spoke his vision about Joseph's life. Joseph's boldness endured, though many people tried to keep him quiet. His boldness resulted in saving the Egyptians from starvation and in reuniting his family. If you asked Joseph before these events why he should be bold, what do you think he'd say? His answer might not be that positive. But, if you asked him at the end of his life why he should have been bold, I imagine he'd have an incredibly wise answer.

When we're trying to be bold, we might not feel like it's worth it. We might not feel that the persecution or the hatred or the suffering is worth obeying God and being bold about it. But we learn from Joseph's life that boldness is both difficult and necessary.

- What persecution in your life keeps you from being bold?
- How can boldness cause persecution?
- Why do we choose not to be bold when we face persecution?

DAY 5

GOD'S WORD

This testimony is true. Therefore, rebuke them sharply, so that they will be sound in the faith.

Titus 1:13

These, then, are the things you should teach. Encourage and rebuke with all authority. Do not let anyone despise you.

Titus 2:15

I pray that you may be active in sharing your faith, so that you will have a full understanding of every good thing we have in Christ. Your love has given me great joy and encouragement, because you, brother, have refreshed the hearts of the saints.

Philemon 6–7

GO

You know, when you talk to your friends about boldness, I bet the conversation goes in one of two directions: being bold for Christ leads to either persecution or persuasion. And somewhere in the conversation someone offers a few stories of both possibilities. You hear stories about people who were seriously persecuted and about people who experienced dynamic results. All from being bold.

Through this week, you've read stories that fall into one of these two categories. But people often leave out a third result that boldness has on others: no response at all.

Your boldness might not get you in trouble, and it might not have any effect on others. Does that depress you? Make you feel like being bold isn't worth it? If your being bold doesn't have any effect on either you or others, why should you be bold? What purpose does boldness have if it isn't effective?

There isn't any passage in Scripture that says, "All believers must live a bold life." God hasn't commanded boldness. It's not an eleventh commandment. But boldness is encouraged. It's a lifestyle that's the result of strong conviction and belief in God. The Bible demonstrates this by telling us about some of the world changers in the early church. For example:

- Paul's boldness was the result of an incredible life-changing experience. His boldness wasn't a choice; it was a result. It was the result of his dynamic encounter with Jesus (check out Acts 9). It caused him to lose credibility with the Pharisees and forced him into a life of both preaching and persecution.
- Peter's boldness was part of his personality. He was naturally outspoken, and standing up for his belief was second nature. Peter's boldness went both ways. He boldly denied Christ and boldly proclaimed him.
- Stephen's boldness came from a strong, solid relationship with God. He performed signs and miracles and was able to debate those who stood against him. The Pharisees ordered him to be stoned, but even while he died, he saw Jesus standing in heaven, and his boldness affected Paul, who witnessed his death and eventually became a Christian. (His story's in Acts 6–7.)

Sometimes boldness results in persecution. Sometimes there are measurable or obvious results. But, more often, our being bold results in small effects in the lives of others. We aren't persecuted, and fifty people don't repent. Instead, one person disagrees with us, or better yet, one person is a little more convinced that they need to trust Jesus.

What should our attitude be when our boldness doesn't have huge results?

We should keep being bold. Timothy, even though he's not known for being bold, had a huge effect on the church in Ephesus. And the Bible doesn't talk about "Titus the Bold," but he was used by God to change the hearts of the people on the island of Crete.

Consistent boldness is a tool in God's hands. If we commit to being bold no matter what the results, God will use our boldness for the glory of his kingdom.

MOVE

- Which is easier for you, one-time boldness or long-haul boldness?
- Which of the two do you think is more effective? Why?
- Why is boldness an important aspect of Christian belief?

DAY 6

GOD'S WORD

Moses answered the people, "Do not be afraid. Stand firm and you will see the deliverance the LORD will bring you today. The Egyptians you see today you will never see again. The LORD will fight for you; you need only to be still."

Exodus 14:13–14

All men will hate you because of me, but he who stands firm to the end will be saved.

Mark 13:13

Whatever happens, conduct yourselves in a manner worthy of the gospel of Christ. Then, whether I come and see you or only hear about you in my absence, I will know that you stand firm in one spirit, contending as one man for the faith of the gospel without being frightened in any way by those who oppose you. This is a sign to them that they will be destroyed, but that you will be saved—and that by God. For it has been granted to you on behalf of Christ not only to believe on him, but also to suffer for him.

Philippians 1:27–29

GO

Christian T-shirts are your favorite thing to own. You've got most of the good ones. The one with pictures of Jesus being crucified, with "He Died for You" on the back in huge letters. Pictures of old wooden crosses with nails and blood on them. You wear these shirts everywhere. And usually people either don't comment on your shirt or they compliment you on your effective witness.

However, today is a different story.

The school security officer approaches you with a really negative look on his face. "You have permission to wear that here?"

"No. I didn't know we needed permission to wear shirts in school."

"Don't be cute with me, kid. Did you read the sign when you entered the school today? You can't wear shirts with messages on them. They're illegal."

"Illegal? Sign? What?"

"That's it, let's visit the principal."

He escorts you to the office, where the principal tells you that Christian T-shirts aren't allowed in school anymore.

You ask the principal what kind of shirts are Christian and why you can't wear what you want to school. The principal gets a little peeved and tells you to watch what you say. He's got a zero-tolerance policy about this issue. Anyone breaking the rules or talking back about this subject will be suspended from school for three days.

"I still don't understand," you begin. "What's wrong with my shirt? I've been wearing these for months."

"It's the message. Some people don't agree, and we don't want to offend them. We want to be careful that school is an open environment where everyone can feel free to express their faith."

"Yeah, but I don't understand. Why can't I express what I believe in?"

"That's it," the principal says. "I don't appreciate you questioning our rules anymore. You're suspended for three days. When you come back to this school, you'll be wearing an acceptable shirt, or you'll get another three days of suspension."

The principal stands up and makes it clear that he's not open to any more discussion. You stand too and walk into the next room, where the secretary is offering you the phone so you can call your parents.

MOVE

- Why do some people believe that Christian T-shirts are inappropriate?

- Are Christian T-shirts really boldness, or are they just shirts that tell people what you believe?
- How does God use Christian T-shirts?

DAY 7

GOD'S WORD

The wicked man flees though no one pursues,
but the righteous are as bold as a lion.

Proverbs 28:1

Now, Lord, consider their threats and enable your servants to speak your word with great boldness. Stretch out your hand to heal and perform miraculous signs and wonders through the name of your holy servant Jesus.

Acts 4:29–30

Therefore, since we have a great high priest who has gone through the heavens, Jesus the Son of God, let us hold firmly to the faith we profess. For we do not have a high priest who is unable to sympathize with our weaknesses, but we have one who has been tempted in every way, just as we are—yet was without sin. Let us then approach the throne of grace with confidence, so that we may receive mercy and find grace to help us in our time of need.

Hebrews 4:14–16

GO

Superheroes come in different shapes and sizes. They can have different superhero powers, different superhero gadgets, and different superhero costumes. But there's one thing that all superheroes have in common. They're all really bold. I mean, what good are superheroes if they can't be bold? It's one of the basic requirements of a superhero. If you can't be bold, then you're just an average, run-of-the-mill Clark Kent or Peter Parker.

So a superhero can't be a superhero without being bold. But could a person who's bold be considered a hero? The answer is *yes*.

To get an idea of the difference boldness can make, try this activity. Go get your favorite book or magazine. (If you've got a comic book, that's even better.) Pick one paragraph or a page out of it to read out loud. First, read it with no inflections in your voice, just completely monotone. Next, read it while shouting or speaking very loudly. Next, read it with feeling and place emphasis on the words that need it. What difference did the various versions make on the way it sounded? Did you understand it differently in the last reading, when all the emphasis was on the right words?

Have you ever read an email that's all lowercase or all uppercase? It doesn't communicate as well, does it? Kind of like what you just read out loud. If you yell everything, no one will want to listen. If you never yell or never make a statement, no one will hear you at all. Boldness at the right moments can communicate so much more.

We should pick and choose the things we want to be bold about. God will help us with these decisions if we give our lives up to his calling and direction. If we're willing to let him decide the message our life communicates, he'll use us in amazing ways. And part of being willing to do that is asking him to help us keep our priorities straight. We should carefully consider what we need to be bold about and stand up for, and what in our lives could distract us from what he wants us to do.

As you consider your life's priorities and what you need to be bold about, remember that above all, you need to be bold about Christ's message of redemption. It will be the greatest superhero work you'll ever do, and when you're open to God's direction, you're never an average, run-of-the-mill person.

MOVE

- What have you learned about boldness from this activity?
- Using what you've learned from this illustration, how would you explain the importance of boldness to your best friend?
- How can you apply what you've learned and the truth you've discovered from Scripture to your life?

Why Should I Live My Faith Now?

DAY 1

Do not boast about tomorrow,
for you do not know what a day may bring forth.

Proverbs 27:1

Therefore do not worry about tomorrow, for tomorrow will worry about itself. Each day has enough trouble of its own.

Matthew 6:34

Now listen, you who say, "Today or tomorrow we will go to this or that city, spend a year there, carry on business and make money." Why, you do not even know what will happen tomorrow. What is your life? You are a mist that appears for a little while and then vanishes.

James 4:13–14

GO

Ever stop to think about tomorrow? I bet you have. Tomorrow is when you have the big exam. Tomorrow is when you play the game against the rival team. Tomorrow is when you expect that important package. The SAT results. An important decision.

You know what? If you live your life worrying about tomorrow, you'll miss some pretty important stuff. You could miss the things God is showing you right now. You could miss moments with friends that can never be relived. You could miss opportunities with your family. So hyperfocused on one thing that you miss what's happening to you right now. What distracts you from noticing the present? What things "in the distance" keep you from focusing on the present?

- _____
- _____
- _____
- _____

Ever heard of "the tyranny of the urgent"? It's the idea that because we're focused on the urgent things, we're never able to think and plan enough ahead. I've got another theory. Sometimes we can be so focused on the future that we actually neglect the present. We don't enjoy what God has placed before us today. Most importantly, we miss the daily opportunities to live for God.

This week we're embracing the present. We're looking at today. There are already loads of people telling you to plan, prepare, and strategize about your future. I'm telling you to embrace the immediate. Live in the moment. And, in all of that, learn to live your faith now. Right now. This very second.

MOVE

- Why is living your faith important?
- What challenges do you face in living your faith?
- What happens to your belief when you commit to live your faith?

DAY 2

GOD'S WORD

Tell the Israelites to bring me an offering. You are to receive the offering for me from each man whose heart prompts him to give.

Exodus 25:2

And here is my advice about what is best for you in this matter: Last year you were the first not only to give but also to have the desire to do so. Now finish the work, so that your eager willingness to do it may be matched by your completion of it, according to your means. For if the willingness is there, the gift is acceptable according to what one has, not according to what he does not have.

2 Corinthians 8:10–12

There is no need for me to write to you about this service to the saints. For I know your eagerness to help, and I have been boasting about it to the Macedonians, telling them that since last year you in Achaia were ready to give; and your enthusiasm has stirred most of them to action.

2 Corinthians 9:1–2

GO

I have a friend who knows the value of living his life in the now. My friend and I used to work in a church together. After youth group, late at night, we'd sit in a car and talk about our lives. We'd talk for hours about how our lives seemed to be going too fast. His comment to me was often, "Sometimes I feel like my life is living me." And I had to agree with him. As Christians, we have to find the balance between always being prepared to help others and not always being exhausted because we're helping everyone, all at once.

My friend demonstrates the value of always being ready. Not with a quick evangelism strategy or anything you might consider super spiritual. He's always ready with his tools. Since he's amazingly gifted with his hands, and he owns a large number of tools, he has the ability to help people with basic house projects.

He's rebuilt the entire interior of a church. He's remodeled other people's houses for them. He's actually helped me remodel parts of my house. He's built countless structures for many people for a variety of reasons. He's always prepared to renovate, remodel, build, and create.

Why?

First, because he has the ability. He examined what he's good at. He thought about what he's passionate about. Then he went out and supported his passion and ability by buying the tools he needed to be the kind of builder and helper he knows God wants him to be. He didn't simply contemplate his abilities; he didn't wait for God to give him a supernatural sign. He examined himself and went for it.

Second, and I think most importantly, because he wants to. It's one thing to have the ability to help people and even have the right tools. It's another to want to help, to take the important step into actually helping them. Thousands of people know what they're good at, but few of them actually use what they're good at to help others. The real challenge of living our faith now isn't just knowing what we can do for others; the real challenge is actually doing it.

Third, my friend relies on God for everything. Here's what I mean. When he's tired from helping others too much, he relies on God to give him the strength he needs to live. When he's helping others and has to postpone things around his house that need to be done, he relies on his friends to help out with mowing the lawn or painting his house.

What are the important keys to living your faith in God right now? First, examine your abilities and know what you're good at. Second, don't hesitate to act on what you know you're good at. Don't wait for some sign from heaven—God wants you to act now. Third, rely on God as your help, sustainer, and support.

MOVE

- What are you good at that you could use to help you live your faith?
- If you hesitate in living your faith, why do you do that?
- What does it mean to rely on God for strength? How do we do that?

DAY 3

GOD'S WORD

"So now, go. I am sending you to Pharaoh to bring my people the Israelites out of Egypt."

But Moses said to God, "Who am I, that I should go to Pharaoh and bring the Israelites out of Egypt?"

Exodus 3:10–11

Moses said to the LORD, "O Lord, I have never been eloquent, neither in the past nor since you have spoken to your servant. I am slow of speech and tongue."

The LORD said to him, "Who gave man his mouth? Who makes him deaf or mute? Who gives him sight or makes him blind? Is it not I, the LORD?"

Exodus 4:10–11

But Moses said, "O Lord, please send someone else to do it."

Then the L<small>ORD</small>'s anger burned against Moses and he said, "What about your brother, Aaron the Levite? I know he can speak well. He is already on his way to meet you, and his heart will be glad when he sees you."

Exodus 4:13–14

GO

What keeps you from living what you believe? Do you feel the urgency to live your faith right now? Are you convinced about the importance of living what you believe and not just talking about it? Are you aware of the things that you're afraid of?

We tend to listen to our deceiving inner voices, don't we? You know these voices, or you at least know their messages. They speak to you when you're feeling bold enough to live your faith openly. They effectively skew the truth just enough to keep us from being bold. What kind of things do they say?

"You're Too Young"

The whisper says, "You can't accomplish anything, because you're too young. No one will take you seriously. No one will believe what you have to say. Don't even try."

You've probably heard the speeches that begin with the passage from 1 Timothy 4:12, where it says, "Don't let anyone look down on you because you are young." The Bible is clear about the capabilities of young people. Your age shouldn't deter you from living your faith.

Too often we hear that we shouldn't allow our age to keep us from living what we believe, but we really don't believe that message. We still don't try to accomplish things, and we rely on adults to do the "big stuff." Living your faith now means you won't rely on adults to do ministry. You can do incredible things for God. Your age shouldn't be a factor.

"You're Not 'Spiritual' Enough"

The whole idea of being "spiritual enough" really confuses me. Some of us wait to live our faith boldly because we think that we don't know enough about God or that we have too many failures to authentically live our faith in God. We feel unspiritual and believe that no one would take us seriously.

Truth is, Scripture is littered with people who lived their faith and wouldn't be considered "spiritually correct" today. David committed adultery. Peter gave up on Christ. You can't wait until you're perfect. You'll never be perfect.

"You Don't Matter"

"The world is a huge place. Lots of people are living their faith. With so many people claiming to be Christians, and with so many people trying to make a difference, you can't really affect the world. Someone more outspoken, more charismatic, more convincing would do a better job." I think this is the enemy's most effective lie. If he can convince us that we won't make a difference or that we can't effectively do the work, then he's won a battle. In fact, this is a battle he won't even have to fight.

Lots of people will tell you that all you need to live your faith is to be bold and forceful and have faith in God. That's true, but you need another thing too. You need to ignore the lies you hear about yourself, your faith, and your ability to live your beliefs.

MOVE

- How does your age prevent you from living your faith?
- How do insecurities prevent you from living your faith?
- What other messages do you hear that prevent you from living your faith?

DAY 4

GOD'S WORD

The quiet words of the wise are more to be heeded
than the shouts of a ruler of fools.

Ecclesiastes 9:17

For you were once darkness, but now you are light in the Lord. Live as children of light . . . and find out what pleases the Lord.

Ephesians 5:8, 10

I urge, then, first of all, that requests, prayers, intercession and thanksgiving be made for everyone—for kings and all those in authority, that we may live peaceful and quiet lives in all godliness and holiness. This is good, and pleases God our Savior.

1 Timothy 2:1–3

GO

Humility is difficult, isn't it? The act of diminishing ourselves for someone else, or even for God, makes us feel as if we're pulling our hair out one strand at a time.

I think we often get humility and humiliation confused. Humility seeks to downplay someone's importance. Humiliation seeks to diminish someone through teasing, joking, or abuse. Humility willingly takes the backseat. Humiliation forces someone into the backseat. Humility desires the best for others.

This is where we get living our faith all mixed up. We get the whole humility/humiliation thing confused. We seek to live our faith boldly and try to do it with all the humility we can gather, and even then we get it wrong. Here are a few beliefs that mess us up:

Living Our Faith Makes Us Spiritual

It's true that living our faith does connect us more to God. However, we're not instantly spiritual when we live our faith. God doesn't necessarily smile on us more. He isn't necessarily more impressed with us. Boldness doesn't necessarily mean that we're more spiritual. Boldness doesn't mean we're more connected to God. Here's the thing though. Many of us who are bold in our faith and aren't afraid to live what we believe tend to carry ourselves like we're more spiritual than others. This isn't true. Living what we believe is a basic requirement of being a Christian. Those of us who do it are just doing what's expected. It doesn't make us more spiritual.

Evangelism Makes Us Spiritual

Do you notice the examples of evangelism that are the most popular and the most prevalent in marketing? The example goes like this: "Jim-Bob is really spiritual because he tells everyone what he believes about God all the time. He's a cut above the rest. You should be like him."

Evangelism isn't spirituality. Evangelism doesn't equal living our faith. Evangelism is either our attempt to tell someone about the change God has made in us (this is what it should be), or it's our attempt at looking hip or cool or smart or even different (this is what it shouldn't be). Evangelism doesn't make us spiritual.

God Is Impressed with Us

For some reason, we believe that our effort and our success at living for God will impress him. Our salvation will be more secure or we'll be more loved by God because we're more devoted than other believers. We believe that how we're witnessing, or how often we're having our devotions, or whatever we're doing to serve God, will impress him. Here's a little wake-up call—God isn't impressed with our attempts to look spiritual. Looking spiritual is empty spirituality.

The key to living our faith is total and complete humility. It's infusing our belief in God with normal living so that others around us are infected by the honest, untainted message that God saves even the worst sinner. We can live our faith trying to be super spiritual or to impress God. In the end, though, those are empty pursuits. Living our faith with real humility marks the world for Christ, and it does so honestly and with a purity that super spirituality can't match.

MOVE

- In what fake ways do you try to impress God?
- How does trying to impress God with our spirituality affect our spiritual integrity?
- Why is living your faith so important?

DAY 5

And we know that in all things God works for the good of those who love him, who have been called according to his purpose.

Romans 8:28

In all my prayers for all of you, I always pray with joy because of your partnership in the gospel from the first day until now, being confident of this, that he who began a good work in you will carry it on to completion until the day of Christ Jesus.

Philippians 1:4-6

May God himself, the God of peace, sanctify you through and through. May your whole spirit, soul and body be kept blameless at the coming of our Lord Jesus Christ. The one who calls you is faithful and he will do it.

1 Thessalonians 5:23-24

GO

History and the people who make history teach us the power of living our faith right now. Throughout the history of Christianity and the formation of the church, heroes dot the landscape. Great leaders and thinkers have sacrificed their lives for the gospel.

For me, there's no greater hero than Francis Asbury. You might not have heard of him. He's not very well known today.

Asbury was a school dropout who lived in America in the early 1800s. He became a Christian and associated himself with the Methodist church. Impressed with John Wesley, the founder of Methodism, Asbury's heart burned to tell people about Jesus. His desire to tell people about Christ led him to pursue what today appears to be a strange kind of occupation. Asbury became a "circuit rider." Circuit riders had an interesting job. They'd ride horses to small, remote communities and preach in the churches there. These rural communities were all over the territory, and men who committed to preach to each church on the circuit had tough jobs. They spent hours alone riding from small town to small town, teaching about God.

This wasn't an easy job. Hours on a horse. Nights often spent sleeping out under the stars. Enduring the weather as they rode. Circuit riders became known not just for the messages they spoke but for their tenacity and their undying commitment to teach and preach the gospel. There was no distance too great for circuit riders to travel. There were no people unworthy of their time. There was no weather too fierce. Their commitment to telling people about Christ was amazing.

Are there people you'd rather not tell about Christ? Is there a distance too great for you to travel? Is there weather you'd like to stay away from? Is there a cost so great that you wouldn't offer yourself? These are the questions we have to ask ourselves when we consider why we should live our faith now. We could ask easier questions, but these are the most important ones, and Francis Asbury helps us ask them.

How uncomfortable are you willing to get for the truth about Jesus Christ? How far are you willing to travel to tell people about him? What are you willing to endure for the sake of the gospel? Does Asbury present a standard too high for us? I don't think so. Asbury offers a real way to live the gospel. He offers us an opportunity to live our faith in a way that makes a real impact.

MOVE

- Why is devotion so important to our relationship to God?
- How does our devotion to God affect the spirituality of others?
- In what ways can you imitate Asbury's passion?

DAY 6

GOD'S WORD

> May he give you the desire of your heart
> and make all your plans succeed.
> We will shout for joy when you are victorious
> and will lift up our banners in the name of our God.
> May the LORD grant all your requests.

Psalm 20:4–5

Commit to the LORD whatever you do,
   and your plans will succeed. . . .
In his heart a man plans his course,
   but the LORD determines his steps.

                              Proverbs 16:3, 9

Many are the plans in a man's heart,
   but it is the LORD's purpose that prevails.

                              Proverbs 19:21

GO

Dinner at the Marshall house is always an interesting event. Ryan's family is a lot different from yours. His parents are a little goofy, a little too happy. Ryan's grandparents live with the family. The house has a too-happy feel with an old-people smell. It makes being there a little strange. Ryan's invitation to dinner came at a great time. Your parents will be gone over the weekend, and you're hungry. You might as well go.

At dinner Ryan's grandfather starts talking. In fact, he begins talking as Ryan's mom is asking what you want to drink, and he doesn't stop talking until you're almost finished with dessert.

The conversation begins with Ryan's grandfather trying to make small talk. He asks you what you're planning on doing with your life. You respond with a simple, "Want to work with people. Maybe a social worker. Maybe a camp counselor or something." But you're just saying anything to answer the question and keep the small talk going.

Ryan's grandfather begins his lengthy speech with, "Ah, people. I remember feeling like I wanted to work with people. . . ." His grandfather talks and talks. Right through the mashed potatoes. Right through the green beans. All the way through his four glasses of milk and a glass of some fiber-boosting drink.

"When I was young, I wanted to work with people. I wanted to be a police officer. I had dreams." And he continues to tell you all his dreams. Every one of them. Each one in detail. Ryan's grandfather goes on and on and then eventually comes to the close of his long speech with a short but very important point.

"Listen to me, young man. I never became a policeman. I never did get to follow my dream. Let me give you one piece of advice. Follow your dream. Don't give up."

After dessert Ryan gives you one of those "let's escape the table" looks. The two of you head up to his bedroom. Ryan tries to gloss over the whole dinner experience with, "My grandfather is kind of old. Sometimes he gets a little weird. I'm sorry for the long story. He's kind of lost it."

"It's cool," you say, still thinking about his grandfather's speech. "Do you think there's something to all of that? Do you think it's okay to follow your dream?"

Ryan seems annoyed that you actually listened to his grandfather. "Uh, I dunno. I know that if I told my dad I wanted to live my dream, he'd yell at me. My grandfather forgets that he made my dad go to medical school. Apparently, he's changed his thinking now that he's ancient."

MOVE

- What advice would you give Ryan?
- Why is living your dream important?
- What prevents you from pursuing an important life goal?

DAY 7

GOD'S WORD

We are therefore Christ's ambassadors, as though God were making his appeal through us. We implore you on Christ's behalf: Be reconciled to God. God made him who had no sin to be sin for us, so that in him we might become the righteousness of God.

2 Corinthians 5:20–21

For physical training is of some value, but godliness has value for all things, holding promise for both the present life and the life to come.

1 Timothy 4:8

We love because he first loved us. If anyone says, "I love God," yet hates his brother, he is a liar. For anyone who does not love his brother, whom he has seen, cannot love God, whom he has not seen.

1 John 4:19–20

Living your faith isn't always easy, but it's also never boring. If you're willing to live what you believe in plain view of everyone you know and even people you don't know, then you're in for a great ride. There's excitement and drama, and something good always comes out of doing it. So you can't lose.

In this devotional, you've been challenged to do lots of different things. So today's challenge is somewhat easier. Go turn on your TV. That's right! Your assignment is to watch TV.

But, as you've probably guessed, that's not the end of it. There's actually a pretty good reason why you're watching TV. You're looking for role models. I don't mean your personal role models. I mean anyone who could be a role model (good or bad) to someone your age. As you flip the channels, you may find athletes, political figures, musicians, actors or actresses, or just famous people. Any of those will work for this activity. Now pick three of them. Write their names down on paper, your *TV Guide*, or your hand, whichever is closest.

Next, consider your answer to this question for each of the three celebrities you've chosen: In what ways are they making the most of their opportunities in life? No matter how you, or even they, may view their careers, being so well known is an opportunity to make a change somewhere in the world. So how are these people making the most of their fame? What direction are they going with it?

Now ask yourself these questions: What would I do if lots of people were watching me on TV? If I were a celebrity, what would change? What would stay the same? I guess your answer to that depends on what's most important to you. If you're into the luxury and money a celebrity often enjoys, that's probably what will drive many of your decisions. But if you're conscious of your status as a role model or a person young people are watching and learning from, then *that* will probably drive more of your decisions.

Of course, we don't need to be on TV to be role models. And we don't need to be on TV to be well known or rich or popular or any of those things. Everywhere we go, people are watching us. When we, as Christians, choose to live out our faith in all aspects of our lives, we're making the most of our opportunities, no matter what we're doing. We're showing them Christ. Living our faith speaks volumes for Christ. That's what we ought to want to do with our lives, whether we're acting on the silver screen, teaching in the classroom, working in a store, or whatever we may do in life. Showing Jesus everywhere is the bottom line.

Want to be a role model? Show Jesus everywhere. And do it now.

MOVE

- What have you learned about living your faith from this activity?
- Using what you've learned from this illustration, how would you explain the importance of living your faith to your best friend?
- How can you apply what you've learned and the truth you've discovered from Scripture to your life?

Tim Baker is a student ministries leader, an adjunct Bible professor, and the author of numerous student books. He lives in Longview, Texas, with his wife and three kids.